ABRAHAM

FATHER OF ALL WHO BELIEVE

Stephen J. Lennox

wesleyan
PUBLISHING HOUSE
wphstore.com

Copyright © 2015 by Stephen J. Lennox
Published by Wesleyan Publishing House
Indianapolis, Indiana 46250
Printed in the United States of America
ISBN: 978-0-89827-904-7
ISBN (e-book): 978-0-89827-905-4

Library of Congress Cataloging-in-Publication Data

Lennox, Stephen J.
  Abraham:Father of all who believe / Stephen J. Lennox.
    pages cm
  Includes bibliographical references.
  ISBN 978-0-89827-904-7 (pbk.)
  1. Abraham (Biblical patriarch) 2. Bible. Genesis--Criticism, interpretation, etc. I. Title.
  BS580.A3L46 2015
  222'.11092--dc23
                            2015001090

To my wife, Eileen, who has helped me
better understand faith—especially faith under fire.

Contents

Acknowledgements	7
Introduction	9
1. The Beginning of the Walk of Faith	23
2. Faith Put to the Test	37
3. Plan B	49
4. Warfare Without and Within	61
5. A Remarkable Conversation	75
6. Coming to God's Rescue	89
7. A Watershed Moment	103
8. Responsible Grace	117
9. Surprising Grace	131
10. God Is Eternal	143
11. No Other Gods	157
12. Behind the Scenes	173
Afterword	187
Notes	199

Acknowledgements

I am grateful to Wesleyan Publishing House for inviting me to write this book and helping to bring it to fruition. Particular thanks to Rachael Stevenson for her assistance. I am also grateful to my wife, Eileen, for her constant support and encouragement.

Introduction

How does one become God's friend? How can one raised among idolaters be redeemed to worship the one, true, invisible God? How does an older man with a barren wife become the father of many nations with descendants too numerous to count? How does a wandering nomad come to inherit the land of Canaan? The short answer: by faith.

This is the story of Abraham, a towering figure in both Judaism and Christianity. His walk with God, described in Genesis 12–25, stands as the hinge on which the rest of the Bible's message turns. Later Old Testament passages remind the Israelites of how God redeemed Abraham (Isa. 29:22) and showed him loving kindness (Mic. 7:20). They recall how, from this one man, God brought forth many (Josh. 24:2–3) and gave the land he had promised (Neh. 9:7–8). They speak of Abraham as God's friend (2 Chron. 20:7). God's work in the life of Abraham gave hope and direction to his descendants.

The Jews living after the Old Testament period continued to look back to Abraham as a pioneer and example (see 1 Macc. 2:52; Sirach

44:19–21). He became the subject of legends (Testament of Levi 6:9; Apocalypse of Baruch 4:4; Enoch 89:10), and the term *Abraham's bosom* was a synonym for paradise (4 Macc. 13:17).

Abraham is often mentioned in the New Testament as well. Stephen retold the patriarch's story in his sermon before the Sanhedrin, and both James and the author of Hebrews referred to him as an example of faith in action (James 2:21; Heb. 11:8–19). For the apostle Paul, Abraham served not only as an example of faith, but also as a linchpin in his argument that salvation comes through faith and not works. In his letter to the Romans, Paul identified Abraham as the ancestor of the Jews and the "father of all who believe" (Rom 4:11).

What does it mean that Abraham is the father of those who believe in Jesus Christ? It signifies that just as Abraham became God's friend through faith, so do we. In what sense, though, does this make him our father? There are at least three ways.

First, Abraham is our father in that he provided the example of living by faith. Those blessed with loving, godly fathers understand how much they learned about life just by watching Dad and then doing as he did. In a similar way, we can learn how we are supposed to believe by paying attention to how Abraham believed. Although there were moments when his faith faltered, on the whole his life provides a commendable example of how to follow God.

This is why the author of Hebrews devoted more attention to Abraham than to anyone else when he provided examples of faith. Abraham demonstrated, sometimes by his failures, that we please God by faith, not by human effort. He illustrated how faith works with, and sometimes beyond, human understanding. Through his example, we see that faith shows itself in deeds, as he constructed altars, hosted God for lunch, and negotiated on Sodom's behalf. We see that faith requires courage, as he left behind Haran, and patience in the decades of delay. His obedient sacrifice of Isaac challenges us to consider the limits of our own faith. Like any good father, Abraham left us faithful footprints to follow.

Second, Abraham is the founder of our faith, the pioneer who charted the path that leads us to God. Americans speak of George Washington as the father of our country because he was instrumental in bringing it into existence. In a similar way, Abraham is the father of our faith. He was the first believer in God's redemptive plan that led to Christ's cross and empty tomb.

When God called Abraham, he promised to bless him and make him a blessing to all nations (Gen. 12:1–3). You might call this passage the hinge of the Bible because upon it swings God's story of redemption. A hinge is made up of two interlocking pieces of metal connected by a pin that allows both pieces to rotate. Think of Genesis 1–11 as one piece, describing the creation and fall of humanity, and Genesis 12 through Revelation as the other, describing how God brought about Israel and the first and second coming of Christ. Abraham is the pin that connects the two pieces.

Throughout the following pages, we will watch God's plan begin to unfold, with Abraham as the central human figure. We will hear God first announce the essential elements of his plan as he calls Abraham to participate. We will hear God promise to give the land of Canaan to Abraham and his descendants and watch as the first plot of that land passes into the possession of God's people. We will watch amazed as God miraculously provides elderly Abraham and Sarah with the son through whom all future descendants would come. Abraham's life and the unfolding of God's plan are inextricably linked.

Even as we see the plan unfold, we catch glimpses of its future. In a vision, God revealed to Abraham what would happen to his descendants in the four centuries that would follow. Abraham's encounter with Melchizedek hints at another, greater priest-king yet to come (Heb. 7). As we view Abraham, a loving father, willing to sacrifice his son for the sake of the plan, our minds cannot help but picture another mountain, another Father, another Son, a greater love, still advancing the same plan.

Because Abraham believed and obeyed, God put his plan into motion, eventually bringing salvation to the Gentiles. As Paul wrote to the Galatians, God "redeemed us in order that the blessing given to Abraham might come to the Gentiles through Christ Jesus, so that by faith we might receive the promise of the Spirit" (Gal. 3:14). Had Abraham not believed and obeyed, God would still have brought salvation, but it would have come in a way that bypassed Abraham. As its pioneer, Abraham is the father of our faith.

A third way Abraham is the father of all believers is as the archetype of those who would come to faith after him. I do not mean merely a hypothetical or symbolic figure; Abraham was every bit as real as you and I. In Abraham's life, however, God provided a picture of what it means to follow him. By watching how Abraham became God's friend, we discover how we can become God's friends as well.

When manufacturers build a new product, such as a car, they start with a prototype, a pattern on which to base all cars of that design. Of course, much of what Abraham experienced does not apply to everyone, for example, his marriage to a barren woman, his nomadic existence, and his material blessings. Yet God intended Abraham's life to be the prototype for future believers, establishing the pattern that all should follow.

As our archetype, Abraham is more than just an example to follow. When we think of Abraham as our archetype and his life as the pattern for all believers, we focus on God and how he arranged the circumstances of the patriarch's life. Examples can be followed or set aside as we determine. We choose to follow Abraham's example when he walked by faith, but we know better than to follow him in his moments of fear. All the people featured in the "Hall of the Heroes of Faith" in Hebrews 11 are examples, but they are not all archetypes. In Abraham we find the prototype of the model believer, a paradigm for every person who wants to have a relationship with God. We can become a friend of God if we follow the pattern marked out by Abraham's life. The word *pattern* derives from the word *father*, so Abraham is our father in that his life marked out the pattern we must follow to become God's friends.

We see this pattern from the very beginning of Abraham's story that began not with Abraham, but with God. Abraham was called to forsake every visible security and follow God. Similarly, your relationship with God does not begin with you searching for him, but with his summoning of you. His command is not to add him to your list of loyalties, but to surrender all your security, deny your-self, take up your cross, and follow him (Mark 8:34). There is no other way to become a friend of God.

As in the case of Abraham, we receive in return for our loyalty a promise (Gal. 3:18, 29). While we may experience some immediate effects from reconciliation with God, most of the promised blessings take time. We must be prepared to wait as Abraham waited. At times God stepped into Abraham's life and revealed a little more of the plan, but most of the time Abraham heard very little from God. Abraham had to hope against reason because some of God's prom-ises seemed too good to be true. God promised Abraham a son through Sarah, though she was barren. He promised him the land of Canaan, although others occupied this land. Similarly, God has promised us wonderful things such as a transformed life, but those things often seem a long way off, if not entirely out of reach.

As we will see in the chapters that follow, Abraham's path was not straight, but it was direct. It weaved over mountaintops and through deep valleys. He vacillated between being God's close friend, someone able to converse with him, and being a stranger who seemed to forget God existed. At times God appeared to be a stranger also, acting in ways Abraham could not understand. However, in spite of this vacillation, Abraham progressed in his walk with God. His trust deepened and his understanding grew until he arrived at the end of his blessed life leaning on the promises that would follow. Although Abraham's own faith was not always what it needed to be, he is the prototype of the true believer, for he demonstrates that we can please God only by faith (Heb. 11:6).

We begin our study of Abraham with his call in Genesis 12 and continue through his death in Genesis 25, learning how he became the example, pioneer, and prototype of our relationship with God. We will give most of our attention to the crucial years that spanned ages seventy-five to one hundred of Abraham's life (Gen. 12:1—22:24), with passing mention of his final seventy-five years (23:1—25:7). Before beginning our study, however, let's briefly consider the historical and literary background of his life.

HISTORICAL BACKGROUND

Abraham lived during the Bronze Age, a time when the cutting edge technology of the day was no longer stone and not yet iron, but bronze, an amalgam of copper and tin. The Bronze Age extended from 3000 to 1200 BC and saw the rise of great civilizations in Mesopotamia and Egypt. Precisely during this time when Abraham lived is not clear, although many argue for a period known as Middle Bronze Age I, from 2000 to 1900 BC. This argument is likely based on the similarity between some of Abraham's practices (for example, his marriage to Hagar) and the customs of the day. Part of the challenge in dating the patriarch's life is that our information about him is limited to what we find in Genesis.

Although Moses likely wrote this material, we will refer to the author as the "narrator." This is not meant to cast doubt on Moses' authorship but to remind the reader that Abraham's story is not a biography like those we might find at the library. It is an ancient history, written by the rules of that day and not ours. For example, modern biographies generally proceed in strict chronological fashion. If they flashback or fast-forward, the author clearly marks this change in time so as not to confuse the reader. This is not the case in ancient history. The author may jump out of chronological order without telling the reader. For example, we learn of Keturah, Abraham's concubine, after Sarah's death (Gen. 25:1–4), but he may have married her much earlier.

Another reason for referring to the author of Genesis as the narrator is to draw attention to these chapters as a literary work. Again, this is ancient rather than modern literature, but we will see many examples of careful structure and literary artistry. Our narrator is divinely inspired but also a product of his time.

LITERARY BACKGROUND

Before telling us the story of Abraham, the narrator provides the information contained in the first eleven chapters of Genesis. In the beginning, God made everything to be very good (Gen. 1–2). The brief picture of Adam and Eve contained in these chapters indicates that humans were created in God's image to reflect his glory, to represent him as stewards of creation, and to experience the blessing of interpersonal harmony like it exists within the Trinity. God's image bearers existed in perfect relationship with him, each other, themselves, and the natural world. All of that changed in Genesis 3, when humanity disobeyed God and ate the forbidden fruit. In place of harmony and peace, there was alienation and pain. Those who had enjoyed unhindered fellowship with God now tried to hide from him. They were at odds with one another and ashamed of their own bodies. Though they once worked in harmony with creation, nature became a harsh reality to be reckoned with.

The alienation that begins in Genesis 3 accelerates through the next three chapters until God pronounces judgment on the mess his very good world had become (chs. 4–6). The story of the flood shows both God's judgment and his intention to continue the human race through a righteous man, Noah (chs. 6–9). God's judgment took place, but it did not solve the sin problem. The disease survived in Noah's family (ch. 9).

Through the account of the flood, the inspired narrator makes several points. First, God hated sin enough to destroy what he had created. Second, God cared about human beings and wanted to preserve them. Third, he also wanted a relationship with humanity; but since he is a holy God, this could only be with righteous humanity. Fourth, even Noah was not righteous enough; the disease of sin was too powerful and pervasive, and by vowing not to flood the earth again (9:15), God eliminated this action as a way of solving the sin problem. He would find a different way.

After a chapter of genealogies, which demonstrates how people once again inhabited the land, the narrator relates the story of the Tower of Babel (11:1–9). This story is more than just an interesting account of human pride and must be understood in light of the problem developed through the preceding chapters. God had created humans to be in fellowship with him, themselves, one another, and nature. Sin then intervened and broke these four relationships, leaving only alienation.

The flood demonstrated both the seriousness and pervasiveness of the disease and God's desire for his relationship with humanity to continue. The story of Babel introduces us to a group of humans employing their gifts to satisfy their desire for fellowship with the divine and to overcome the alienation that marked their lives. God had endowed them with the gifts to harness nature for the purpose of serving their ends, but they employed those gifts to construct a tower. This tower was likely a ziggurat or artificial mountain meant for worship. Their aim was both to worship God as they understood him and to preserve the fellowship of their community. This too was something good, another aspect of the divine image. They were also trying to make a name for themselves and replace their feelings of self-doubt with honor and glory. Those who built the Tower of Babel were trying to regain what they knew they needed. Humans may drift far from God, but they cannot escape the desire for harmony with God, one another, themselves, and nature.

If the tower builders were seeking to restore what they had lost, why did God put a stop to their efforts? He did so because those efforts were doomed to failure. The builders would have experienced mastery over the natural world, built a great tower and city, and experienced great pride in their accomplishment. Yet the momentary sense that they had found what they were looking for would soon have dissipated and they would have kept looking for another way to satisfy their restlessness. God put a stop to the Tower of Babel not because humans were aiming for the wrong goal but, because they would have had just enough success to blind them to the reality that the curse of sin remained.

God is too merciful to allow us to experience satisfaction in anything less than the best. He knew the builders of the tower needed to understand that the fruit they truly sought hung well beyond the reach of any humans, even gifted ones. God dismissed Adam and

Eve from the garden so they could not eat from the Tree of Life and thereby made permanent their alienation. He did the same at the Tower of Babel, scattering the builders so they could not reach the dead end of perceived success.

Abraham's life can be understood only in light of the story of this unfinished tower. Although they hungered for what had been lost, humans were unable to find it on their own. Only God could solve the sin problem, which is precisely what he began to do with Abraham. While those who sought to build the tower began from their sense of need, God began his solution by summoning Abraham. Reconciliation would not be gained by human arms reaching up, because our arms are too short. It could come only when divine arms reached down. The plan of those at Babel seemed so right and looked so impressive. God's plan, by contrast, seems ridiculous: promise an old man with a barren wife descendants too numerous to count. However, by using the foolish to shame the wise, God builds faith and weakens pride. Those at the Tower of Babel sought to find their security and significance in the collective and familiar, but God knows that security and significance can be found only in him. This usually means separating us from other emotional supports. The tower builders sought a good goal through self-centered means, while Abraham's call, right from the start, was to be a blessing to others. God's plan solves the problem left unsolved by Babel, but it also solves the problem created by Babel, the scattering of all nations into separate languages, loyalties, and customs. God's promise to bless all nations through Abraham was eventually fulfilled in Christ, and it removes all dividing walls of hostility (Eph. 2:14).

It is possible that neither the author of Genesis nor Abraham himself fully comprehended the reach of God's redemptive plan. Even so, the Holy Spirit continued to reveal this plan to the other authors of the Old and New Testaments. From Abraham and Sarah, an elderly, childless couple, God created the people of Israel, then liberated them from Egyptian slavery and formed them into a nation through the Mosaic law. This nation received land in Canaan and then a leader in King David. At their best moments, the people understood that God had called them to be a "light for the Gentiles, that [their] salvation may reach to the ends of the earth" (Isa. 49:6). Through God's work among them "all the ends of the earth will remember and turn to the LORD, and all the families of the nations will bow down before him" (Ps. 22:27).

Because of their disobedience to this call, the people of Israel experienced the purging effects of exile and foreign domination. The time came, however, when this nation produced the Anointed One whose life, death, and resurrection became the means through which "all peoples on earth [would] be blessed" (Gen. 12:3). In one of his sermons, the apostle Peter spoke of how "beginning with Samuel, all the prophets who have spoken . . . foretold these days" (Acts 3:24). He told the Jews gathered before him: "You are heirs of the prophets and of the covenant God made with your fathers. He said to Abraham, 'Through your offspring all peoples on earth will be blessed'" (3:25). When Paul was describing to the Galatians how salvation had come to the Gentiles, he spoke of Abraham, citing Genesis 12:3: "Scripture foresaw that God would justify the Gentiles by faith, and announced the gospel in advance to Abraham: 'All nations will be blessed through you.' So those who rely on faith are blessed along with Abraham, the man of faith" (Gal. 3:8–9). Peter and Paul represent the conviction of the early church that Jesus had come to fulfill the promises God had made to Abraham.

The Gospels relate the crucial moment when God himself became flesh and dwelt among us in the person of Jesus. His teaching and miracles provided a glimpse of the promised kingdom where God would rule over a reconciled realm, a realm that became reality through the death and resurrection of Christ. That reality began small but grew during the days of the early church, as we see in the book of Acts and the Epistles. Through the work of the Holy Spirit, all people were blessed with the gospel. The church was instrumental in spreading this message and was itself an example of this reconciliation.

The book of Revelation provides a glimpse of the fulfillment of God's redemptive plan. Through Christ's work, the people of God will come to experience new life in a world free of sin's alienating effects. In his vision of the New Jerusalem, John saw humanity reconciled with God. "The throne of God and of the Lamb will be in the city, and his servants will serve him" (Rev. 22:3). The visionary saw no "temple in the city, because the Lord God Almighty and the Lamb are its temple" (21:22). There will be no sun or even a lamp, for "the Lord God will give them light" (22:5).

John saw humans reconciled to each other, with city gates that never close (21:25) no more tears (21:4), or anything shameful (21:27). Finally, he saw humanity reconciled to nature, for "there will be no more death or mourning or crying or pain" (21:4) and the leaves of the Tree of Life will be for the "healing of the nations" (22:2). John described what will take place when "the old order of things has passed away" (21:4) and there is "no longer . . . any curse" (22:3).

CONCLUSION

The plan that triumphantly comes to fruition in the New Jerusalem began with Abraham in the city of Ur. The plan would unfold gradually, even imperceptibly, but without pause. There was apparent culs-de-sac and detours, but the plan continued to unfold. From its beginnings in

Ur, it would travel to Canaan, then Egypt, the wilderness, back to Canaan, and for a while in Babylon. Finally it would reach Bethlehem and then, Jerusalem, specifically Golgotha, the tomb, and the upper room. After that it raced on to Judea, Samaria, and the uttermost parts of the earth.

All of this lay in the distant future. Long before Abraham became the father of those who believe—our example, pioneer, and prototype—he was living with his family in Ur, far from the land of Canaan and even farther from faith in the one true God. That is, until God spoke to him.

1

The Beginning of the Walk of Faith

GENESIS 12:1–9

The first eleven chapters of Genesis describe a very good world that became very bad because the virus of sin corrupted it. Even the large-scale destruction of the flood could not eradicate sin's widespread effects. Humans cannot ignore the sense that they are alienated from God, others, themselves, and the natural world. One group sought to provide the reconciliation they knew they needed by building a city and tower. Their efforts were doomed not because they could not build such a city but because they could. Apparent success would have blinded them to the fundamental alienation that would have certainly remained.

Then God inaugurated a plan that was certain to succeed, though to all appearances it looked like an utter failure. According to this plan, Abram would need to learn to walk by faith, a faith that would test him to the core. In doing so, Abram became our example, pioneer, and prototype in God's long-term process of reconciling humans to him, each other, themselves, and nature.

FOLLOWING BY FAITH (GEN. 12:1–3)

According to Genesis 12:1, God commanded Abram to leave his country, people, and family and go to a land that Yahweh would show him. This appears to be the second time Abram had received these instructions. According to Stephen's version of these events (Acts 7:2), God first spoke to Abram while he was in Ur. This scenario also fits God's statement that he had taken Abram from Ur of the Chaldeans (Gen. 15:7) and the recollection of later Israelites (Neh. 9:7). This initial call likely led Abram to leave Ur and head toward Canaan by way of the city of Harran. His wife Sarai, nephew Lot, and father Terah, accompanied him (Gen. 11:31). For some reason they traveled no further than Harran. Both Ur and Harran were centers of worship for the moon god Sîn. Perhaps the idea of leaving behind familiar religious convictions may have been too much for Terah to contemplate. Abram also stayed, perhaps out of a similar fear, perhaps out of respect for his father, or perhaps due to the mistaken notion that his call depended on his father's attendance.

Some believe Terah was alive when Abram received his second summons. If Terah fathered Abram when he was seventy years old (11:26) and Abram left at age seventy-five (12:4), Terah would have been 145 at his son's departure and lived another sixty years until he died at age 205 (11:32). More likely, God's second call came at the time of Terah's death. Genesis 11:26 could be read to mean Abram was born at some point after Terah was seventy. Otherwise, we would have to conclude that all three of Terah's sons were born in his seventieth year. If Abram was born when Terah was 130 and left seventy-five years later, his departure would have been when Terah was 205. Although we cannot always determine the order of events from the order of their appearance in Hebrew narrative,

Terah's death is mentioned before Abram's call. This would explain why God did not command Abram to leave his father, only his "father's household" (12:1). It also seems the simplest way of understanding Stephen's assertion in Acts 7:4: "After the death of his father, God sent him to [Canaan]."

We do not know how God called Abram the first or the second time. The text only says that God spoke to him. The calls may have come in a dream or vision or through an angelic messenger. However they came, they conveyed to Abram three important facts. First, he must continue his journey to Canaan. Second, the God issuing this command was not one of the gods he had been raised to worship. Third, Abram learned that Yahweh, was patient and persistent.

In our highly mobile culture, families often live in separate parts of the country so we can easily miss the great sacrifice Yahweh asked of Abram. It was no small thing to leave one's homeland, even accompanied by one's father. It was especially hard to leave behind both country and father, and head off into the unknown. During that time, one's identity was tied to one's country and family. Leaving these meant taking on a new identity and giving up the security and stability found in extended family. A person's religion was largely determined by geography, with certain gods associated with specific regions. To leave one country and go to another meant crossing into the lands of other gods.

God was aware of these concerns and seemed to word his command to intentionally challenge them. He began by commanding Abram to leave his country, something he already had agreed to do when he departed Ur. "Your people" refers to Abram's "relatives" (NASB) or clan (Gen. 12:1). God commanded him to leave behind those who were like him, who shared a common lineage and were responsible to look out for him, and for whom he was responsible. The screws tightened further with the words "your father's household" (12:1). Abram could no longer remain with his closest kin.

God's next command may have been the most challenging. Abram was to go to the land God would show him (12:1). Very likely, Abram already knew this land was the country of Canaan, since God revealed this in the initial summons (11:31). With this command, God did more than summon Abram to go to Canaan. He commanded him to adopt a new lifestyle that required Abram to move whenever and wherever Yahweh said. Abram would no longer be a city-dweller as he had been all his life. He would become a nomad. City-dwellers looked down on nomads in those days. Those who lived in cities, especially important cities like Ur and Harran, enjoyed many advantages, such as ready provision and protection. To give up city life and wander at the direction of an invisible God was no easy assignment.

God's summons also meant a change in what it meant to be religious. Yahweh, a God Abram had most likely not previously worshiped, had summoned him. The old ways of relating to the gods—sacrifices, magic, omens, divination, prophecies—had brought some sense of protection from the unpredictable supernatural realm. God's summons brought all this into question. Yahweh demanded that Abram expose himself to the unknown and dangerous spiritual forces he had previously worshiped. His only security would be found in carefully listening for Yahweh's direction and obeying when it came.

God's command to Abram, our archetype, is the same demand he makes of each believer. In the words of a German martyr, Dietrich Bonhoeffer, "When Christ calls a man, he bids him come and die."[1] To follow God, we must die to our preferences and privileges, our security and stability, our loyalties and loves. "No one who puts a hand to the plow and looks back," said Jesus, "is fit for service in the kingdom of God" (Luke 9:62). The only way to experience friendship with God is to die to self.

God followed up his command with a series of promises meant to replace the security Abram had been commanded to surrender (Gen. 12:2–3). God's promised Abram that he would be made into a great nation, blessed, and given a great name that would provide him with an identity far greater than what he had left behind. Others would be blessed by blessing Abram and cursed when they cursed him. The whole earth would be blessed through him. Abram was asked to believe that being the fountain of such blessings would provide all the security he would ever need.

However, before he could take hold of these promises, Abram needed to let go of his previous identity and security. God demands our surrender before he provides his blessing. He commands us to follow before showing us the route. In Abram's case, God promised so much blessing that the whole world would be abundantly supplied from the overflow. In our case, no one who leaves behind "home or wife or brothers or sisters or parents or children for the sake of the kingdom of God will fail to receive many times as much in this age, and in the age to come eternal life" (Luke 18:29–30).

The blessings God promised were invisible to Abram at the moment of his call, and most would remain so throughout his lifetime. He would see his family, household, and possessions increase, but he would not live to see his descendants become a great nation. He may have lived long enough to hear someone bless him- or herself in his name, but Abram would not live to see all peoples of the earth blessed through him.

Although the fulfillment of these promises was not visible to Abram, the promise represented a reality more precious than anything he was being summoned to surrender. The obedience God commands is costly and hard; the path of faith is dark. Yet such sacrifices fade to nothing in light of what he has promised us: "a new heaven and a new earth" (Rev. 21:1).

Some promises are made to obtain a quid pro quo, something for something. We promise to pay back a loan because we need something the money will buy, such as a car or house. Yet God never makes promises so he will obtain something.

We sometimes make promises as gifts to another person, such as wedding vows. These promises are not made in exchange for something, but are gifts given based on a commitment to the other person. These are the promises God makes. Abram, not God, would gain everything from this relationship. Even more astounding, God initiated this relationship out of his grace and mercy upon Abram and all of his spiritual descendants. His relationship with God, like ours, results entirely from divine grace.

Let's examine more closely God's seven promises (Gen. 12:2–3):

1. "I will make you into a great nation."
2. "I will bless you."
3. "I will make your name great."
4. "You will be a blessing."
5. "I will bless those who bless you."
6. "Whoever curses you I will curse."
7. "All peoples on earth will be blessed through you."

God's first promise was to make Abram into a great nation. Abram likely thought that because Sarai was barren God could provide descendants in other ways. He may have assumed these would come through his nephew Lot. After Lot's departure, Abram designated his servant Eliezer to be his heir (15:2). When Abram learned that his descendants would come through his own seed, Abram assumed that would be accomplished through other wives or concubines, such as Hagar (ch. 16) and perhaps Keturah (25:1–4). When God informed Abram that the child would be Sarai's, Abram and his wife found this first promise laughable (17:17; 18:12). It seemed like a joke to them, but it would not be the last time God would employ a barren wife in his nation-building process. Of the next five women involved in producing this family, three were barren: Rebekah (25:21), Leah (30:9), and Rachel (30:1). Only Bilhah and Zilpah, slaves like Hagar, were able to bear children without divine intervention. Apparently, God was not interested in using the most sensible plan to accomplish his purpose but the one requiring the most trust. God was building not merely a great nation through Abram; he was building a great people of faith.

The specifics of the first promise are illuminating. The Hebrew language has several words that describe a large group of people. The word used here refers to a nation, like the nations mentioned in Genesis 10 or the nation of Egypt. Although *nation* is singular in chapter 10, the promise would later be expanded so that Abram became the father of many nations, including the Ishmaelites and Edomites (17:4–6, 16, 20; 25:23).

The second promise was God's blessing on Abram. We are not told all that this blessing involved, but it certainly included the many descendants God had promised (22:17). This blessing did include material prosperity. In Genesis 24:35, "blessed" informs us that God had made Abram rich in "sheep and cattle, silver and gold, male and female servants, and camels and donkeys." God made Abram rich through a variety of means, including natural and supernatural, and by plundering the Egyptians (Ex. 3:22).

God's third promise was to make Abram's name great and expand his reputation. This promise is similar to the one God gave David (2 Sam. 7:9). Abram's name would become widely known, and he would be respected as a man who enjoyed God's favor. More than once Abraham's neighbors would comment on this favor (Gen. 21:22; 23:6).

God's fourth promise was that Abram would become a blessing to others as his prosperity and reputation spilled over to enrich the lives of those around him. Abram's name would be proverbial for a blessed person; others would say, "May you be as blessed as Abram." This is another way Abram serves as our archetype. As his life was characterized by blessing, so can ours as we claim Jesus' Beatitudes as our own.

The fifth and sixth promises assured not only that Abram would be blessed, but also that his blessings would be contagious. God promised that those who blessed Abram would find themselves blessed and those who cursed Abram would themselves be cursed. The first word rendered "curses" in Genesis 12:3 implies treating someone or something in a dismissive or contemptible fashion, such as ridicule, mocking, or derision. The second word used for "curse" has a more serious connotation. It implies that those who harmed Abram would experience even greater harm. Those who ridiculed Abram would become ridiculous, those who dismissed Abram as insignificant would lose their own significance, and those who wished evil on Abram would find an even greater evil on their own heads.

God leaves no doubt about who will bring about these results: "I will bless . . . I will curse" (12:3). Naturally, this would mean an increasing number who bless Abram and a shrinking number who curse him. More encouraging than the promises of prosperity and protection is the assurance that God himself is watching out for his friend Abram.

The seventh and final promise was that "all peoples on earth will be blessed through" Abram (v. 3). Some suggest that instead of "will be blessed," the verb should be rendered "will bless themselves," but God had already promised something very close to that ("you will be a blessing"). It seems unlikely that God's culminating promise would merely reiterate something he had said earlier. Instead, they build upon one another. These blessings would flow indirectly from Abram, depending on how others treated him. In this final promise, Abram learned that blessings would flow through him directly to "all peoples on earth."

The phrase "all peoples on earth" is literally "all families of the ground." The word *families* suggests something broader than nations or peoples (see Gen. 10:5, 18, 20, 31–32). *Ground* may have been chosen rather than "world" or "earth" to allude to the curse God had placed on the ground in consequence of human sin. This final promise was specifically intended to reverse this curse.

As I suggested in the introduction, Genesis 12:1–3 is the hinge of the Bible. Before this passage, the story had been about humanity spoiling God's good work of creation. Upon these verses, the Bible swings from the problem to the solution. In these three verses particularly the last phrase of verse 3, we encounter God's plan to remove the curse of sin. The rest of the Bible unfolds the fulfillment of this plan and points to its consummation at Christ's return.

All of this began with Abram. He was the pioneer of God's redemptive plan. What started at Ur ends in the New Jerusalem. The damage done in the garden of Eden began to be undone through Abram before concluding in another garden, Gethsemane. We are Abram's children not only because we believe as he believed, but also because our pioneer provided us with the opportunity to become God's friends.

Genesis 12:4 may be one of the most surprising verses in the Bible. With so much to lose, so little guaranteed, and so few of his questions answered, "Abram went." Abram knew very little of the God who made these promises. He did not know exactly where he was going or what he would encounter when he got there. He had the bare minimum of information, just enough to get him started out of the gates of Harran.

Welcome to God's school of faith. He will make clear his will for you, but it will be step-by-step. You will be told just enough to hold you accountable but not enough to allow you to operate independently of his help. You will be expected to do what God commands simply because God commands it. You will always have more questions than answers. You will be better acquainted with what obedience costs than what it procures. You will need to let go of your security and trust yourself to an invisible God who expects you to lean on his promises. Those promises will seem as unlikely as a great host of descendants coming from an infertile couple.

ABRAM ARRIVED IN CANAAN (GEN. 12:4–9)

One commentator suggests Abram would have proceeded south from Harran through Damascus, along the northern shore of the Sea of Galilee toward Megiddo, then south to Shechem, a journey of nearly five hundred miles.[2] Shechem, located near the present-day city of Nablus, was well off the main roads, so one wonders why Abram would choose to travel there.

The narrator provided several clues that suggest Abram first headed to a well-known sacred place in Canaan. Abram headed not just to Shechem but specifically to the "site of the great tree of Moreh at Shechem" (v. 6). The term "site" could also be translated "holy place." Many in the ancient world considered trees to be particularly suited as places of worship (Deut. 12:2). This was not just any tree; it was "the great tree," probably one marking an especially sacred spot. The name Moreh likely comes from the Hebrew verb meaning "to teach." Perhaps this tree was known as a place for instruction or even for obtaining oracles, just as Deborah obtained oracles at a palm tree (Judg. 4:5).

Why did Abram travel to this site? Having arrived in Canaan, he may have wondered what to do next and assumed the best place to hear from God was at a site famous for divine oracles. Or Yahweh may have directed him to this site to lay claim on this territory, much as an army might plant its flag on newly conquered land. In Abram's case, it was not a flag but an altar that he left behind (Gen. 12:7). Since Yahweh was establishing a new way of relating to himself, an altar was the better symbol of conquest. Another possibility is that Yahweh led Abram there as a concession to his assumptions about how and where God would reveal his will. Whatever the reasons for Abram's arrival at the great tree, Yahweh appeared to him there, but not with further direction. He gave Abram another promise: this land would belong to the patriarch's descendants.

This marks the first time Yahweh is said to have appeared to Abram; earlier he had only spoken to him (see 12:1). We are told of his appearing to Abram only two other times (17:1; 18:1). This incident is significant because it is the first time God revealed his intention to give the land of Canaan to Abram's offspring. Earlier God had directed Abram to Canaan and promised to make him a great nation (12:2). Now he made it clear where this nation would settle. This is the first time God would reveal his plan one piece at a time. Abram and all his spiritual children would need to get used to the gradual manner in which God reveals his will. The narrator let us know that Israel's acquisition of Canaan would not be easy, because "at that time the Canaanites were in the land" (12:6). God gave this promise to Abram and at the same time revealed the need for the patriarch to be patient, walk by faith, and wait on God to do the impossible.

Abram left Shechem and headed south for about thirty miles. He stopped between Bethel in the west and Ai in the east. We do not know if this was another well-known sacred spot or just a good place to pasture his flocks and herds. Once again Abram built an altar, and for the first time Abram "called on the name of the LORD" (12:8). This phrase may describe Abram at prayer, or it could refer to an act of worship (see 4:26). A third possibility is that Abram made some form of proclamation. This is the sense in which this same verb is used in Exodus 33:19, when God promised to proclaim his identity to Moses. If this last understanding is correct, Abram chose this location as an occasion to declare his faith in Yahweh to those who lived nearby. That he did so only after following his God for a short while displays Abram's courage, a trait we will see often.

From this location near Bethel, Abram continued south until reaching the southernmost point in Canaan, the land of the Negev (Gen. 12:9). God had directed him to Canaan and promised this land to his offspring. Abraham responded by traversing Canaan from north to south. In a sense, he laid claim to the land by faith. How and when God would remove the Canaanites, Abram did not know. He still did not know how God would fulfill any of the promises he had made. Abram had much to learn about walking with Yahweh, but to his credit and our eternal benefit, he stepped out by faith and not by sight.

CONCLUSION

Abram's call was all about faith. He received and responded to that call by believing that he must trust God and take action. He stepped away from all that brought security and identity, trusting himself entirely to God. This walk of faith was actually part of something bigger than Abram, something that would impact every person who would ever live and every inch of heaven and earth. By issuing this call, God inaugurated his reconciling plan through Abram, the pioneer. As Abram walked by faith, he became our example.

But faith requires more than good beginnings. Having left Harran and arriving in Canaan, Abram had to learn to follow One who does not always lead by the shortest, safest, or clearest route. His first lesson was about to begin as God allowed famine to devastate the land he had promised to Abram's descendants.

2

Faith Put to the Test

GENESIS 12:10–20

The first nine verses of Genesis 12 present Abram as a hero of faith, courageously turning his back on his security and identity out of obedience to God. If those verses present Abram at his best, verses 10–20 may present him at his worst: fearful, self-serving, forgetful of all God had promised, and oblivious to his moral responsibilities. While the decline from the mountaintop of faith to the valley of fear is steep, it should not be unexpected. Abram's experience reminds us that significant testing often follows spiritual high-water marks. Immediately after Jesus' baptism, divine words of affirmation were still ringing in his ears when the Spirit sent him into the wilderness of temptation. Jesus passed that test with flying colors, but not all God's servants do as well.

Before Abram could become the father of all who believe, he had much to learn about God, himself, and faith. God's purpose in the painful and humiliating experiences described in verses 10–20 may have been to help Abram learn these lessons. Abram was shown the power and seriousness of sin, especially in his own life, and God helped him see how faith works and why it is essential. In this test, Abram was able to learn more about the character and power of the God he followed. Abram also saw that, in spite of his sin, he remained God's chosen instrument.

ABRAM IN EGYPT

Famines are especially dangerous in a subsistence economy like ancient Canaan's, and the famine experienced during Abram's time was severe. Famines usually occurred as the result of warfare, pests, crop failure, or drought. Had the cause of this famine been any of the first three, Abram probably could have relocated to an unaffected part of the country. Given that he left Canaan altogether and moved to Egypt, we could assume that this famine resulted from prolonged drought.

Canaan is entirely dependent on rainfall and dew for its water supply. Its main river, the Jordan, flows most of its length in a deep ravine, making it essentially useless for irrigation. Rain falls only from October to May and often comes in heavy downpours that run off quickly rather than ground-soaking showers. The inhabitants of ancient Canaan learned to direct this precious moisture to cisterns, holes in the ground often plastered with limestone, thereby preserving the water for later use.

If the rains failed to come, disaster followed. Crops withered in the fields and food prices soared. Societal ties could unravel as people migrated or turned to violence to stay alive. Since a wealthy nomad like Abram could protect and provide for his family longer than most, the famine must have been severe to make him leave Canaan for Egypt. Abram may have considered Egypt a long-term destination, for the text speaks of him going "to live there for a while" (12:10).

The path from Canaan to Egypt was well traveled in times of famine because of Egypt's ever-present water supply, the Nile River. One ancient Egyptian source speaks of a time when Egypt was "crushed by the weight of these starving herders."[1] An inscription from a fourteenth-century Egyptian tomb describes such a migration: "Certain of the foreigners who know not how they may live have come. . . . Their countries are starving and they live like the beasts of the desert."[2] Later, God would forbid Abram's son, Isaac, to make this trip (26:2). During another famine, he would send Joseph ahead of his family to preserve Abram's descendants from a later famine (50:20). This time God neither commanded nor prohibited Abram's journey.

In Abram's day, Egypt was already a well-established civilization, nearly two thousand years old. The Pyramids of Giza had stood glittering in the sun for centuries, the Great Sphinx for a millennium. Egyptian traditions and beliefs were deeply ingrained and were blossoming into their classic expression during the Middle Kingdom Period. At the pinnacle of this culture stood the pharaoh. He was not only absolute ruler, but was also regarded as divine. To experience his favor ensured blessing; to arouse his anger invited disaster.

As Abram approached Egypt, he was probably less frightened of Pharaoh than he was of ordinary Egyptians. He feared that one of them would become so smitten by Sarai that he would make her first a widow and then a wife. Some find it strange that a woman in her sixties could be that beautiful. Keep in mind that Sarah lived until she was 127 (23:1) and so was just approaching middle age at this time. The rabbis considered Sarah one of the four most beautiful women in the Bible, along with Rahab, Abigail, and Esther. Remember, too, that beauty is a cultural value. What the people of one culture or era consider gorgeous might be grotesque in another.

As it turned out, Abram's fears for his safety were justified. The Egyptians considered Sarai beautiful. Egyptian records indicate at least one instance when a husband was killed so someone could marry his beautiful wife. However, we do not see Abram turning to God for protection or asking God for advice. Instead, he concocted a scheme that put himself, his wife, and God's plan in jeopardy. He instructed Sarai to call herself his sister, explaining, "I will be treated well for your sake and my life will be spared because of you" (12:13).

If Abram had any hesitation about his plan, he may have rational-ized that this was at least a half-truth; Sarai was his half sister. They shared the same father but not the same mother (20:12). Abram might have thought that by calling Sarai his sister he was not only protecting himself, but also providing an opportunity for escape. Any marriage to his "sister" would have required negotiations over the terms of the arrangement. While the terms were under discussion, Abram and his family would have had a chance to slip out of the country.

Abram intended this plan to protect him from the average Egypt-ian, but he did not consider what he would do if Sarai attracted Pharaoh's attention. When the king's officials praised the beautiful sister of a wealthy foreign nomad, Pharaoh decided to add her to his harem. As pharaoh he had no need to negotiate for his new wife. All he had to do was lavish Sarai's "brother" with valuable and abundant gifts such as "sheep and cattle, male and female donkeys, male and female servants, and camels" (12:16). The last item was especially generous because these "ships of the desert" were only then becoming widely domesticated.

Abram's plan lay in shambles. No negotiations meant no oppor-tunity to escape. Sarai was suddenly gone, and Abram found himself in a lose-lose dilemma. He could go to Pharaoh, explain what he had done, and return the generous bride price, but the consequences of his confession would likely be disastrous. To do so would make Pharaoh look foolish and expose the Egyptian monarch to danger. Ancient Egyptians were very religious and considered taking another man's wife an invitation to incur the anger of the gods. Abram's other option was to do nothing, thereby losing his wife and putting God's promises in jeopardy.

He chose to do nothing, so God did something. Stepping into the mess Abram had made, God "inflicted serious diseases on Pharaoh and his household" (12:17). The Hebrew word "diseases" is used in Exodus to describe the plagues God sent on the Egyptians. It is also used to describe a skin disease or a spot of mildew that might appear on clothing or a wall (Lev. 13:2, 47). Some have argued that God afflicted Pharaoh with some kind of skin disease, like boils. The rabbis believed the king and his nobles were stricken with leprosy and were unable to have sex.[3]

The seriousness of the illness and the fact that it extended to his household would have convinced Pharaoh that he had somehow offended the gods. To discover what this offense was, he would likely have consulted his advisors and the Egyptian priests. Perhaps Pharaoh realized that the problem had begun when Sarai entered the palace. He may have questioned her and learned the truth. Another possibility is that God confronted Pharaoh in a dream, as he would do to Abimelek under similar circumstances (Gen. 20:6–7).

However discovered, the truth made Pharaoh furious. All-powerful monarchs do not take it lightly when they are humiliated and subjected to divine reproach. Pharaoh had the power and motive to kill Abram, but he had discovered that Abram's God was more powerful and was protecting him. To harm this man would have exposed Pharaoh to a punishment worse than what he had already experienced. His frustration is palpable in his questions to Abram: "What have you done to me? . . . Why didn't you tell me she was your wife? Why did you say, 'She is my sister,' so that I took her to be my wife?" (12:18–19). Abram said nothing in reply. Perhaps he was speechless with shame, or perhaps Pharaoh gave him no opportunity to respond. The king dismissed Abram after sputtering, "Now then, here is your wife. Take her and go!" (12:19).

Pharaoh ejected Abram not just from his court, but also from Egypt. He deported Abram with an Egyptian escort. To Pharaoh, Abram was particularly dangerous because he served a powerful god. This was not the kind of person Pharaoh wanted hanging around. He may have thought, "Let him keep the bride price. It is better to lose livestock and slaves than risk offending his god. Abram must leave my country, but I must not drive him out by force and risk more divine punishment. I will send some of my officials and soldiers to escort him to the border. That way I can be certain he is out of my hair."

What must Abram have been thinking as he hurriedly put his household in traveling order and began the journey north? He had entered Egypt voluntarily but fearful of the Egyptians. He was now leaving under compulsion because the Egyptians feared him. He had entered Egypt to preserve his household but had nearly lost it. Now he was leaving in disgrace, unsure of what lay ahead. Imagine his shame at having to leave Egypt under official escort, fearfully wondering how he and his family would find food and water in famine-ravaged Canaan. Picture him wondering what his failure had done to God's promises.

This sorry episode in Abram's life is riddled with evidence of sin's corrupting effects. Famines happen in a fallen world. Abram's fear and shame arose because sin alienates us from ourselves. Sin also leads to interpersonal alienation, such as the conflict between Abram and Pharaoh. Abram's failure to trust or even consult God is the kind of thing that happens when humanity is alienated from its creator. Whether or not Abram fully understood what was happening, we can see clear evidence of sin's alienating effects in this episode.

The narrator makes a similar point with Noah (chs. 7–9). God sent a flood to destroy a world saturated with sin, sparing only righteous Noah and his family. But this did not solve the problem of sin. We soon see that even those who disembarked from the ark carried the disease. Noah became drunk, and Ham dishonored his father (9:20–25). Abram may have been the pioneer of this plan of redemption, but someone else would need to bring it to perfection (see Heb. 12:2).

This story also demonstrates the mercy and power of a God who has committed himself to eradicating sin. In the midst of a world torn by alienation and in spite of the disobedience of God's chosen pioneer, God still delivered him. An even greater deliverance came to Abram's descendants who were captives in Egypt. Many have noted the similarities between Abram's experience in Egypt and that of his descendants centuries later. Both entered Egypt because of a severe famine, and both were "captured" by Pharaoh. Both demonstrated a lack of faith in God's ability to deliver them, Abram by not trusting in God's promises, and the Israelites by not believing that God had sent Moses and Aaron (see Ex. 5:20–21; 6:9). Deliverance came for both through plagues. When they left, both Abram and the Israelites plundered the Egyptians (Gen. 12:16, 20; Ex. 12:36).

Abram's deliverance anticipated the Israelites' deliverance which in turn anticipated the greater deliverance brought about through the cross and the empty tomb. Complete freedom will arrive when Christ returns to finally and forever break sin's death-grip on God's world. Like Abram and the Israelites, our sojourn as strangers here will end, and we will return to our homeland. On that day, we will not be driven out in shame by an angry king but will, with deepest joy, "meet the Lord in the air. And so we will be with the Lord forever" (1 Thess. 4:17). The author of Hebrews put it this way: "Since the children have flesh and blood, he too shared in their humanity so that by his death he might break the power of him who holds the power of death—that is, the Devil—and free those who all their lives were held in slavery by their fear of death. For surely it is not angels he helps, but Abraham's descendants" (Heb. 2:14–16).

Because Abram's experience in Egypt was a personal defeat, it teaches us little by way of example. We can, however, still learn from his experience. As the archetype, Abram's life serves as the pattern for what it means to follow God. First, we see that the solution for the sin problem lies beyond our reach. If even the pioneer of the plan needed redemption, each of us does as well.

Second, Abram's experience demonstrates how easily we can come to rely upon ourselves rather than on God. Perhaps after the heady experiences of Genesis 12:1–9, Abram imagined himself as God's gift to humanity, immune to temptation and invincible against attack. Discovering our weaknesses, learning what terrifies us, and realizing how easily we stumble are not pleasant lessons, but they are bitter mercies from a gracious God. Nor do we always learn such lessons easily. Abram needed a refresher some years later when tempted with a similar situation (see ch. 20).

Third, our archetype teaches us that faith is developed through testing. Tests might arise from circumstances beyond the control of any human power, as did the famine; a fallen world provides plenty of problems. Testing also might follow from a person's own mistakes. Abram's lie about Sarai only made matters worse, and as Abram would later discover, sometimes God himself brings the test.

However the tests arise, past success is no guarantee of future success. Faith is not like currency that can be banked once it is earned.

Faith is more like a muscle that must continually be exercised. Ever-increasing weight and resistance are what develop faith's tone and power. One step of faith makes it necessary to take another step. The faith that caused Abram to leave Harran's ample water supplies led him to a land prone to drought and famine. Abram's exercise of faith in leaving behind his family in Harran and launching out alone made him more vulnerable when he entered Egypt. This experience taught Abram and his spiritual offspring that the decision to act in faith must be a daily decision.

Perhaps the famine and his new-found vulnerability raised doubts in Abram's mind about God's reliability. It was God, after all, who had led Abram to a place troubled by famine, and it was God who separated him from the protection of the extended family in Harran. It was God who had given him a gorgeous wife and remained silent when a word of direction would have made all the difference. But no comfort or direction, not even correction, came down from heaven. Abram heard no words of reassurance during the severe famine. When he decided to go to Egypt, God said nothing to stop him. When Abram hatched his cowardly scheme, God was mum, allowing Abram to blunder his way into a dangerous situation. Why was God silent? It may have been for the same reason that a classroom teacher remains silent when an exam begins. A test is not a time for instruction but a time to see what the student understands. In a true test of faith, there is always the freedom to fail.

Abram did not do well on this test because he attached too much importance to his circumstances and too little to God's promises. God had assured him that he would father a great nation, have a great name, and be a source of blessing to others. Surely this implied God's guarantee of Abram's provision and safety. Yet God's promises seemed to fade with Abram's fears. When forced to choose between making judgments based on current circumstances and trusting God's promises, we should always choose the latter.

One problem with basing decisions on circumstances is that we do not know which circumstances are the most important. What appears to be very important in any given moment might be trivial in the long run, while seemingly trivial details may actually be very important. Apparent danger is not always real danger, and real danger sometimes hides in the most benign things. For example, if a barking dog frightens you, you may walk quickly in the opposite direction. What you may not see is that the dog is chained and the pavement is covered with ice. Trying to escape the harmless dog, you injure yourself by slipping on the ice.

So too, Abram misjudged the real danger in his situation. He saw the famine in the Promised Land as a disaster, even a reason to doubt God. The famine was, in fact, an opportunity to seek God's direction and trust God's provision. Abram feared the Egyptians in general and Pharaoh in particular, not realizing that God had put them on a short leash. Abram feared those who were harmless but ignored the One he should have feared. Instead of looking to God for protection and provision, Abram looked to himself.

The consequences of this choice could have been disastrous. By lying about Sarai, Abram put himself and his wife in mortal danger. Had Pharaoh insisted on retaining Sarai as a wife, Abram would have been forced to choose between remaining close to his spouse or returning to the Promised Land. Decisions based on fear of circumstances rather than faith in divine promises inevitably lead to lose-lose situations. Centuries later, the rebellion of the Israelites would leave them wandering, unable to return to Egypt but ineligible to enter Canaan. During the conquest of Canaan, Israel made a treaty with the Gibeonites without consulting God. As a consequence, the Israelites were forced to choose between dishonoring

God by breaking the treaty or disobeying God by allowing the Gibeonites to live (see Josh. 9). From Abram's failure, we learn that by fearing God we eliminate the need to fear anything else, and we protect ourselves from self-inflicted disaster. Faith is strengthened through times of testing, during which God may be silent. At such times, we must completely trust in God's promises and character, not our circumstances or our strength.

The fourth and last lesson to learn is that God can turn our failures into something good if we allow him to do so. Although Abram had to experience the consequences of his choices, God protected him from the worst. He received back his wife, both their lives were spared, and they were able to continue in God's plan.

By bringing good from our failures, God shows that he is motivated by his sovereign grace, not by what we deserve. God protected Abram because Abram was his chosen servant, not because Abram was the most righteous person in this story. God kept his promise to "curse those who curse" Abram, because God always keeps his word. Although the Bible teaches the possibility that our willful rebellion can put us outside the reach of salvation, we should not underestimate the length of God's arm.

God redeems our mistakes and transforms those mistakes into blessings. Abram left Egypt richer because of Pharaoh's lavish gifts. Being forcibly expelled from Egypt was a moment of great shame for Abram. At the same time, it was God's way of getting him out of Egypt, where he didn't belong. God plucked Abram from Egypt, where Abram had thought he could make a life, and planted him back in Canaan, where he would find his destiny. God's sovereign grace turns all things, even our mistakes, into our good and his glory (see Rom. 8:28).

CONCLUSION

Although the sojourn in Egypt was not an easy experience for Abram, it provided an opportunity to learn important lessons about God, sin, faith, and himself. And God taught all this without uttering a word. Only those who live by faith can learn such lessons. How else does one learn from divine silence? Some time later God spoke to Abram again, but only after Abram experienced yet another test of faith, this time involving his nephew, Lot.

3

Plan B

---◆◆◆---

GENESIS 13

We often say that God has a wonderful plan for our lives, and of course he does. What we don't like to say or sometimes think about is that for God to accomplish his wonderful plan, he must first abolish our plans. We must be willing to surrender our plan A and accept his plan B, even when his plan does not seem as good as ours, takes longer than ours would have, or when the plan is only the promise of a plan.

Abram had a plan A, a clear idea of how God would fulfill all the wonderful promises he had made. Genesis 13 is the story of how God removed Abram's plan A and replaced it with his own plan B. Or more precisely, how God replaced Abram's plan A with the promise of plan B. In time God would demonstrate the superiority of his plan, but in the meantime, Abram would need to walk by faith.

ABRAM AND LOT SEPARATED (GEN. 13:1–13)

Abram did not return to Canaan empty-handed. One might have expected that the severe famine would have depleted his livestock. Instead, Abram returned "very wealthy in livestock and in silver and gold" (13:2). The narrator emphasized Abram's wealth by describing it with the same adjective he used to describe the famine (12:10).

Abram returned to Canaan still married. Specifically mentioning that Abram returned with his wife is important because he almost lost her to Pharaoh's harem. Increased wealth in the face of natural disaster and the preservation of his family in spite of his cowardice were both a result of Yahweh's faithfulness. God was keeping his promises.

Abram first traveled to the Negev in the south of Canaan, then north to an earlier campsite near Bethel. His reasons for traveling to these specific places are unclear. He may have been intent on recapturing the initial clarity he knew after his call, either through restless wandering or by intentionally retracing his steps. If he was retracing his steps, it seems odd that he did not return to Shechem because it was there that Yahweh had appeared to him and first promised the land (12:6–7).

Abram may have traveled first to the Negev in search of grazing areas for his abundant possessions. The Negev was not the most fertile of Canaan's regions, but Abram may have thought it sufficient for his animals. However, Lot, who was traveling with his uncle, also possessed great flocks and herds, and it seems that the Negev could not supply water and pastures for both men's animals. Abram may have reasoned that by leaving the Negev and moving to a more fertile region, he and Lot could remain together. Abram knew of such a place where he had previously camped, so they headed north.

Eventually they arrived where they had lived before the famine. By mentioning that Abram settled between Bethel and Ai, the narrator seemed to suggest that Abram intentionally avoided populated areas. Tracing Abram's path through Genesis shows that he traveled primarily between less populated sites in the central mountain range of Negev and avoided the more populated coastland, the region of Galilee and the Jordan Valley. Perhaps he sought to avoid the sinful activities that characterized the land's inhabitants (see 13:13). He was looking for a space large enough for him and his nephew to remain together with all their livestock. Lot was likely Abram's designated heir, so he wanted to remain close.

Earlier, Abram had built an altar at this place and "called on the name of the LORD" (12:8). Upon his return, he once again "called on the name of the LORD" (13:4). Whether praying, worshiping, or proclaiming, Abram's experiences in Egypt must have given him a clearer picture of his God. If he was praying, Abram now understood the importance of calling on God for guidance and courage in order to avoid disastrous choices. If Abram was worshiping, it must have been with a fuller sense of his own unworthiness and of God's grace in rescuing and restoring him. If calling on Yahweh means Abram was proclaiming the truth about his God, his proclamation must have been with a deeper sense of confidence in the Lord's ability to fulfill his promises.

God used Abram's experiences in Egypt to expand his understanding of what it means to walk by faith, and he will do the same for Abram's spiritual offspring. God will use our experiences—both good and bad—to clarify, refine, and deepen our devotion to him. He is able to make our worship the edifying combination of our daily challenges and his gracious sovereignty.

Even in the better pasturage of the highlands, Abram and Lot discovered that "the land could not support them while they stayed together" (13:6). The herdsmen of Abram and of Lot argued over access to grazing lands and water (13:7). The narrator chose this moment in the story to point out that Canaanites and Perizzites inhabited this land (13:7). The presence of other groups increased the competition for land.

Yet Abram did not want to part from Lot. Since the death of Lot's father, he had become more like a son to Abram. Perhaps Abram and Sarai had legally adopted Lot as their heir. This would explain why he accompanied them when they left Harran. When God promised them numerous descendants, Abram and Sarai likely assumed these would come through Lot.

Eventually the overcrowding became intolerable, leaving Abram no choice. He approached Lot and suggested they part ways. As uncle, surrogate parent, and protector, Abram had the right to direct Lot to the territory he would receive. Instead, he approached Lot, calling him a brother for whom quarrelling was totally out of place. Abram was both humble and generous in giving Lot first choice. If Lot chose to go south, Abram would go north (13:9). Lot's answer likely surprised Abram, since he chose not south or north but east, toward the plain of the Jordan.

In many ways, Lot's choice was a good one. The almost oval-shaped alluvial plain, nearly twenty miles wide, was well watered, thanks to the Jordan River and a large aquifer. This land was great for planting and grazing. Wheat, barley, dates, olives, grapes, figs, pistachios, almonds, and flax grew there in ancient times.[1] The narrator compared it to "the garden of the LORD" and "the land of Egypt" (13:10). The first phrase probably alludes to the garden of Eden (2:8–14; Isa. 51:3). The narrator compared this plain to the land of Egypt because both were lush and well watered. According to Deuteronomy 11:10, irrigating a field in Egypt was as simple as dragging your foot through the sand.

The narrator had a second reason for mentioning Egypt. It appears Lot's experience in Egypt had spoiled him. Earlier, he had lived in a well-watered land during his years in Mesopotamia. Then his visit to Egypt with Abram reminded him how nice it was to have a ready supply of fresh water. Lot seemed to have grown tired of Canaan, a land so heavily dependent on rain.

While Lot's choice made sense on one level, it was deeply troubling on another. Lot's preference for a ready water supply revealed a reluctance to walk by faith. His choice of land was still in Canaan, but the land lay at Canaan's very edge. With time, Lot would move farther and farther from the land of promise. When last we see him, he is living in the mountains above Zoar outside Canaan. He and his offspring had forfeited any share in Canaan, instead receiving Moab and Ammon as their inheritance (Deut. 2:9, 19).

Lot's choice was also troubling because it led him to pitch his tents near Sodom. This was unwise in two ways: first, an aside mentions the coming judgment on Sodom and Gomorrah (Gen. 13:10; 19); second, Sodom was inhabited by "wicked" people, who were "sinning greatly against the LORD" (13:13). To call the Sodomites wicked is enough to raise concerns about Lot's choice. The second phrase alerts us that the sins of the Sodomites were in defiance of Yahweh, who was fully aware of what was happening there.

GOD APPEARED TO ABRAM (GEN. 13:14–17)

After Lot's departure, God spoke to Abram. The narrator opened this section by emphasizing that Yahweh had waited until this moment to speak again. God saved these reassuring words about Abram's descendants and the land until after Lot left.

God began by instructing Abram to "look . . . north and south, to the east and west" (13:14). In his comments to Lot, Abram had alluded only to the land to the south and north (13:9), but God mentioned all four cardinal directions, broadening Abram's vision. He promised to Abram's descendants "all the land" the patriarch could see (13:15). This included the land Lot had chosen. What Abram had graciously given away, God returned.

God added the words "that you see" (13:15) to what he had promised Abram earlier. When in Shechem, Abram was not able to see the extent of the land that now lay before him as he stood near Bethel. God repeated and expanded his earlier promise, adding a visual aid to boost Abram's faith.

God added something else to his earlier promise. This land was not only for Abram's descendants but for Abram as well: "to you and your offspring" (compare 13:15 with 12:7). In this way, God assured Abram that the promise was not for the distant future only; it was a promise for his own lifetime as well. God made a third addition to his earlier promise by using the word *forever*. This let Abram know that the land that stretched before him would belong to his descendants for a long, long time. Abram lived and died in this land without taking full possession of what had been promised. He obtained a well (21:22–34), a field, and a cave (ch. 23), but he paid for them. Though the land belonged to Abram by divine promise, he was not allowed to possess it.

Earlier, God told Abram he would become a great nation, implying many offspring. Now God emphasized this large number by adding another visual aid. They would be like the "dust of the earth" (13:16). Just as no one can count all the particles of dust in the world, Abram's descendants would also be too many to count.

Throughout Abram's life, God often renewed and expanded earlier promises, but why did he do so at this moment? God's timing may have something to do with Abram's recent experiences in Egypt. Hearing from God after a lengthy silence would have encouraged Abram. Hearing these predictions would have been especially heartening because they assured Abram that God's earlier promises remained in effect. God expanded them in spite of Abram's failures. God's gracious words would have banished any lingering self-doubt in Abram's mind.

It also seems that God spoke these words in response to Abram's generosity. Earlier Abram had gotten himself into trouble by thinking only of himself (12:11–13). God's words now affirmed Abram's self-lessness. The man who put his wife in jeopardy to save his own neck had willingly given the advantage to his nephew. How different from the frightened patriarch we met in the last chapter. There he worried about the Egyptians, in part because he was entering their country without the protection of extended family. Later, he courageously parted company with his extended family. Abram seemed more con-vinced of God's promised protection and provision. Perhaps God's appearance at this moment was meant to affirm Abram's growing trust.

At this time, Abram was probably confused about who would be his heir. He had assumed it would be his nephew, but this was unlikely after Lot's move toward the margins of Canaan and the town of Sodom. Abram likely perceived Lot's disinterest in God's promises and his uneasiness with the life of faith. Abram's plan A was fading as Lot's figure receded to the horizon of Canaan. The question of plan B loomed in his mind. God chose this moment to speak. In his reaffirmation and expansion of earlier promises, God assured Abram that he did indeed have a plan B, though it was not yet time to reveal it.

Instead, God reiterated his promises by telling Abram to "walk through the length and breadth of the land" he was being given (13:17). God may have been telling Abram to inspect the land, or he may have been commanding Abram to begin to acquire the land. To walk about a land's length and breadth was legal language for the act of acquiring it. The problem with these possibilities is that nothing was said about Abram either inspecting or acquiring the land, only that he moved to a place near Hebron (13:18). Most likely Abram understood God's statement not as a command but as a divine land grant. He could inspect the land if he wished, but he would not need to acquire it; God would see to that.

When discussing Genesis 12:6, I suggested that sites sacred to the land's inhabitants were often marked by trees. By settling and building an altar near the great trees of Mamre, Abram may have been proclaiming to the Canaanites: "I know you worship your gods here, but I have come to tell you about the true God, Yahweh." Abram would spend a considerable period of time at Hebron.

The events of this chapter provided Abram, the pioneer of God's redemptive plan, with ample evidence that such a plan was necessary. The men of Sodom who were "sinning greatly against the LORD" (13:13) graphically illustrates humanity's alienation from God. Humanity's alienation from nature is evident in the inability of the ground to support the livestock. Sin also causes conflict among humans as evidenced by the disputes among the herdsmen of Abram and Lot.

If Abram sought to overcome some of the effects of alienation by moving from the Negev to Bethel, his efforts only prolonged the inevitable. His only solution for stopping the interpersonal conflict involved personal separation. This separation was necessary but also made it easier for Lot to make unwise decisions regarding where he would live. All of this may have left Abram feeling frustrated.

Yet even this frustration was part of God's plan. Abram needed to learn that, although he was the pioneer of God's reconciling work, only God could solve the sin problem. Abram needed to trust

God to do what Abram could not do. God did not object to Abram's attempts to improve the situation and probably wanted Abram to do what he could. Later God even involved Abram in Sodom's judgment (see 18:16–19). God was pleased with Abram's efforts but not surprised by his failure. As at the Tower of Babel, God sometimes allows our frustration lest we imagine we have succeeded rather than failed.

Abram is the father of believers because he provides an example of how to believe. In this episode, his example contrasts sharply with Lot's. The two men illustrate the difference between walking by faith or by sight. When Lot began to examine the terrain, he "looked around" (13:10). God used an almost identical wording when he told Abram to "look around" (13:14). The narrator contrasted two ways of looking. Lot saw a well-watered land and chose based on what he had seen. Abram saw the land currently occupied by others, but instead of trusting what he saw, he put his faith in God. Lot drifted to the border of Canaan where less faith was needed; Abram remained in the heart of the land where he would need to depend on God. Lot inched along the wicked cities of the plain; Abram remained separate from the surrounding culture.

Abram "made his home in the promised land like a stranger in a foreign country" (Heb. 11:9). He built altars to Yahweh and called on his name as a demonstration of his trust in God's promises. "He lived in tents . . . looking forward to the city with foundations, whose architect and builder is God" (Heb. 11:9–10). Lot started out living in tents near Sodom (Gen. 13:12), and before long he would leave his tents and take up residence within the city itself (ch. 19). This was not a matter of God preferring country dwellers to city dwellers. God loves all people, wherever they live. The contrast between Abram and Lot was between walking by faith and walking by sight, between settling for an earthly Eden and waiting for what

God has promised. When Lot looked, he saw his Eden and set out to possess it. When Abram looked, he saw a land he owned but did not possess, a land requiring faith. He remained in that land, waiting for God to fulfill his promise. In the end, Lot's Eden turned out to be only Sodom, while Abram's faithful patience made him "heir of the world" (Rom. 4:13), the father of those who believe. As it was with the father, so it will be with his spiritual offspring: They walk by faith.

Abram's walk with God serves as the paradigm or prototype for all believers. From these events, we see why it is so important to walk by faith. How else but by faith can we follow a God who is so often silent? Abram had heard nothing from God since he was in Shechem, which was before the famine, the trip to Egypt, the return to Canaan, the conflict between the herdsmen of Abram and Lot, the decision to give Lot first choice, and Lot's departure. Because God was silent, Abram had to solve these problems on his own. At times he chose well, as when he gave Lot first choice. At times he chose poorly, as in Egypt. God remained silent in order to give Abram the opportunity to exercise his moral freedom. As we know from raising our own children, we must tell them what to do but allow them to put our instructions into action. When they internalize our instructions so that their actions reflect both their will and ours, we call that maturity. God's silence means that we must live by faith and walk in obedience to the light he provides.

Another reason God remained silent was to demonstrate his ability to work through Abram's decisions, the good ones and the bad ones. We see that God was more faithful to his promises than Abram was to God. Abram had to suffer for his foolish choices regarding Sarai, but God showed his willingness to forgive and provide another chance. Abram still had lessons to learn, but he never again took God's mercy as a license for carelessness.

While God was silent, he was working behind the scenes. He advanced the redemptive plan by returning Abram to Canaan. The geographical focus of God's plan was not Egypt, so God removed Abram from where he did not belong and redirected him where he was supposed to be. Earlier, God had promised Abram material blessings. As Genesis 13 opens, God returned Abram to Canaan "heavy" with livestock and riches. In doing so, God demonstrated his ability both to carry out his promised blessings and to abundantly bless in the face of famine, all the while saying nothing.

This period of God's silence was a great time to develop faith. Hearing nothing, Abram had to act on what he knew about God's character and plan. He did not always make the best choices, but the tension created in the absence of clear divine direction strengthened his faith muscle. Faith began when God spoke, but it grew best in God's silence. Abram's spiritual children must learn this lesson as well.

Eventually, God did reveal himself to Abram (13:14), but not until Abram had stepped out in faith. Faith is not a crowbar to pry open God's clenched fists, nor is it a magic word that charms God into giving us what we want. God is sovereign and acts according to his perfect will. However, faith demonstrates our submission to his will and our trust that he "rewards those who earnestly seek him" (Heb. 11:6).

When God revealed himself to Abram, he reaffirmed and expanded his earlier promises by adding two visual aids to reinforce them: the panoramic view of the land and the dust of the earth. In this way, God made it easier for Abram to believe. At other times, God calls his people to walk in the dark. Yet, most of the time, God graces us with confirming words, whether from another believer, circumstances, or directly from Scripture.

God could have told Abram everything all at once, but instead he revealed his promises here and there. In this way, Abram learned that following God required him to walk in obedience. Stepping away from God risked missing a part of what God had in store. The apostle James reaffirmed this truth for all believers when he wrote, "Faith without deeds is dead" (James 2:26).

CONCLUSION

At the beginning of Genesis 13, Abram returned to Canaan with great wealth, an intact family, and a keener sense of God's power. He probably also arrived with an idea of how God would fulfill his promises—plan A. By the chapter's end, plan A has moved away and settled near Sodom. Abram's nephew, Lot, was replaced not by another person but by the promise of plan B. Abram seemed content with the exchange. He was satisfied to remain a stranger in his own land, trusting Yahweh for what lay ahead. Abram could not have anticipated the challenges before him or the surprise encounter that would follow.

4

Warfare Without
and Within

GENESIS 14

Genesis 14 is the only chapter in Genesis that brings Abram or the other patriarchs into the focus of international events. While we cannot identify with certainty all the participants and locations mentioned here, the narrator clearly intended to convey that Abram lived in a dangerous world. However, Abram's faith throughout his adventures allowed him to emerge safely and stronger in the end.

ABRAM TO THE RESCUE (GEN. 14:1–16)

The land God had promised to Abram was perhaps the most strategic stretch of real estate in the ancient Near East, serving as the only land bridge connecting Europe, Asia, and Africa. Large and powerful nations to the north and south fought to control this land bridge while the smaller kingdoms in Canaan were forced to either defend their independence or make alliances. The opening twelve verses of Genesis 14 provide the first reference to warfare in the Old Testament, a campaign fought by the Elamites and their allies that included a battle with some of the kings of Canaan.

To refer to these Canaanite rulers as kings could be misleading because their territory was essentially confined to a single city with its surrounding villages. Their strength came through alliances such as the one we see here. The Canaanite city-states included Sodom, Gomorrah, Admah, Zeboyim, and Bela. Admah and Zeboyim, first mentioned in Genesis 10:19, suffered the same fate as Sodom and Gomorrah (compare Deut. 29:23; Hos. 11:8). We see Bela in Genesis 13:10, mentioned by its later name, Zoar. All five cities were located near the Dead Sea. Bela was likely at the southern end of the sea, but scholars are unsure whether to locate the other four cities there or at the northern end of the sea.

Several factors favor the north. First, Lot chose to occupy the large plain that sits north of the Dead Sea according to Genesis 13:10. A parenthetical comment in that verse associates this plain with Sodom and Gomorrah where Lot pitched his tents.

Second, the northern coalition marched up the northwest shore of the Dead Sea as far as Hazezon Tamar (14:7), at or near En Mishpat, before engaging the Canaanite kings in verse 8. If Sodom and Gomorrah were south of the sea, that would mean the enemy forces marched past these cities on their way north, thereby leaving themselves exposed to attack from the rear. More likely, the enemy coalition defeated En Mishpat and then continued north to where Sodom and Gomorrah were located.

Third, archaeologists have found the remains of a sizeable city northeast of the Dead Sea. This city had an elaborate gate (compare 19:1) and was utterly devastated by a fiery conflagration toward the end of the Middle Bronze Age (1600 BC), a time period that fits with the likely time of Abram.[1]

For a dozen years, these Canaanite kings had been subject to Elam, located in what is now Iran until they rebelled. The Elamites joined forces with several other kingdoms (14:1–4). Shinar is better known to us as Babylon, although we know nothing of a Babylonian king by the name of Amraphel. His name appears first in the coalition, though the rebellion was against the Elamites, suggesting the importance of Babylon in the region. Ellasar could refer to eastern Asia Minor (now eastern Turkey) around Pontus or Cappadocia, or a town between Carchemish and Harran, near where Abram had begun his journey.[2] The former is more likely, since Ellasar is mentioned before the actual organizer of this military campaign, Kedorlaomer, king of Elam.

As this powerful coalition marched south, they conquered territory on the eastern bank of the Jordan River (14:5–7). They defeated Ashteroth Karnaim (14:5), a location known from sources outside the Bible as well. They continued south as far as the Sinai Peninsula, likely reaching what is now the city of Eilat. Next, they turned back northwest toward Kadesh. From Kadesh they continued north along the western shore of the Dead Sea until they reached Hazezon Tamar (14:7), likely En Gedi or a wadi a few miles to the north.[3] This sweeping military venture subdued the Rephaites, giant-like inhabitants of the northern Transjordan region (compare Deut. 2:11, 20; 3:11, 13; Josh. 12:4; 13:12), as well as other inhabitants of these territories. This detailed list of conquests may seem unrelated to the story of Abram, but it conveys the military might of the coalition, making their defeat at the hands of Abram that much more striking.

Finally, the Elamites and their allies arrived in the Valley of Siddim, just north of the Dead Sea (Gen. 14:3, 8), where they faced off against the rebellious Canaanite kings. When the Canaanites were routed, they scattered for their lives (14:10–11). This area has long been known for its tar or asphalt, and the battle site, as one translation describes it, "was one bitumen pit after another."[4] The Dead Sea would later be called Lake Asphaltitis. In the ancient world, bitumen was used for mortar in building construction (Gen. 11:3; Ex. 1:14) and as sealant for boats (Gen. 6:14) and baskets (Ex. 2:3).

In their hasty retreat, some Canaanites either fell into these bitumen pits or jumped in to hide from the enemy; others fled to the mountains. The northern coalition then plundered Sodom and Gomorrah (Gen. 14:11). Lot, by now a resident of Sodom, was taken prisoner and all his possessions were seized (14:12). We do not learn the fate of the rest of his family, although mention of women among the spoils suggests Lot's wife and daughters were also captured (14:16).

"Abram the Hebrew" was living near Hebron (14:13), about forty miles from the site of the battle. This is the first time in the Bible anyone is labeled a Hebrew. The term may refer to the descendants of Eber (11:16–27), or it may refer to troublesome nomads.[5] The term *Hebrew* appears most often in international contexts such as the story of Joseph, the events of the exodus, and the conflict with the Philistines. Occasionally the Israelites referred to themselves by this term, although always when distinguishing themselves from non-Israelites. Whatever the narrator's reasons were for calling Abram a Hebrew, it distinguishes the patriarch from both the northern invaders and the southern kings.

News of Sodom's fall reached Abram by means of one who escaped the battle. Why he came to Abram is unclear, given the distance between Sodom and Hebron. Perhaps Lot, anticipating the fall of Sodom and his capture, sent a messenger to Abram with a plea for help. Abram responded immediately by enlisting the assistance of the local Amorite chieftains who were "allied with Abram" (14:13). This phrase, used only here in the Old Testament, implies that Abram signed a pact with these men for mutual benefit and protection. They had another reason to participate. As Amorites, they could avenge the mistreatment of other Amorites by the northern coalition.

Abram also mustered 318 men of his own household. This number might seem small to us, but based on battle accounts from the ancient Near East, this constituted a sizeable force. The verb *called out* might be translated literally as "poured out" or "emptied out," suggesting Abram embarked on an immediate and thoroughgoing rescue mission for Lot. These men are described as both "trained" and "born in his household" (14:14), meaning ready for battle and loyal. Credit goes to Abram for the foresight to prepare this militia even before the threat appeared. The ability to enlist more than three hundred men suggests that Abram's total household would have numbered in the range of a thousand. God was indeed blessing Abram!

Abram immediately headed north and encountered the enemy near Laish, later known as Dan, about 135 away miles away. Abram divided his forces and attacked at night, sending the northern coalition into a panic. He then pursued the retreating enemy for nearly fifty more miles. The rout was so complete that Abram recovered all the plunder and captives, including Lot, before turning south (14:14–16).

The picture of Abram in this episode is unlike anything we have seen up to this point. It reveals his courage, strength, and cunning. As soon as he learned of Lot's plight, Abram sprung into action. He had a simpler option: He could have paid a ransom for Lot's safe return. Captives in the ancient Near East were sometimes kept as slaves, but a wealthy man like Lot would more likely have been redeemed by relatives at a hefty price. Abram could surely have afforded the ransom and would have experienced much less effort and risk. Instead, he expressed his loyalty by immediately mustering a militia and pursuing the enemy in a week or more of hard marching.

The nighttime attack was risky. Likely facing a larger opposing force, Abram divided his forces to create the impression of size. He could not have known whether the enemy was anticipating such an ambush. This is the kind of man you want beside you in difficulty: courageous, daring, and fiercely loyal.

ABRAM AND TWO KINGS (GEN. 14:16–24)

On Abram's return trip, when he was about twenty miles from home, two kings met him. One had traveled up from Sodom; the other had come from Salem (Jerusalem), where he ruled. These two kings met Abram in the "Valley of Shaveh" (14:17), likely near Siloam where the Kidron and Hinnom valleys meet. The narrator contrasted these two kings with the king of Salem bringing food while the king of Sodom came empty-handed. Other than food, Melchizedek, the king of Salem, offered only a blessing while the king of Sodom was prepared to offer Abram even greater wealth.

We see the king of Sodom first (14:17). We know his name was Bera (see 14:2), but the narrator chose not mention it here, probably as an intentional slight. When we last saw this king, he had either jumped into a tar pit or hid in the hills while running from the northern coalition (14:10). The narrator made it seem as if the king had been hiding in the pit this whole time, coming out only when the fighting ended. Whatever the king of Sodom had been doing, Abram did the opposite by risking his life to pursue the enemy.

Next we meet the king of Salem, Melchizedek (14:18). We learn he was a priest, the first person designated with this title in the Bible. The story of Melchizedek captivated the ancient Israelites. Psalm 110 refers to him as the ideal king, who led God's people with power and piety. Fascination with Melchizedek continued among Jews after the Old Testament period. He was mentioned in synagogue prayers during the Hellenistic period.[6] The community of Jewish monks that produced the Dead Sea Scrolls expected Melchizedek to play a significant role on God's behalf in the last days. One Jewish work from the first century spoke of Melchizedek's birth and removal to the garden of Eden until he becomes head of all future priests.[7] Compared to Jewish speculation, the treatment of Melchizedek in Hebrews seems tame (Heb. 5:5–10; 6:20; 7:1–22).

Melchizedek brought bread and wine, perhaps as part of a sacrifice or to feed Abram and his men or both. Salem appears to have been unaffected by the northern coalition, so Melchizedek's gift arose not from gratitude but from spontaneous kindness. Melchizedek not only fed Abram, but also blessed him in the name of the deity whom he served as priest, El Elyon, or God Most High. El was the name of the chief god in the Canaanite pantheon, considered the god of the earth, while Baal was the god of heaven. Melchizedek did not appear to be worshiping this El, since he described his God as "Creator" or possessor of both "heaven and earth" (Gen. 14:19).[8] Melchizedek not only blessed Abram by El Elyon, but also credited El Elyon with giving Abram victory over the northern coalition (14:20).

At some point, Abram came to the startling conclusion that Yahweh, the God he worshiped, and El Elyon, worshiped by Melchizedek, were the same God. Our first clue is when Abram gave Melchizedek a tenth of the spoils (14:20). The tithe rightly belonged to the deity who had given Abram the victory. By giving this to Melchizedek, Abram acknowledged that Yahweh and El Elyon were the same God. A second clue that he equated the two is when Abram called his God "Lord, God Most High, Creator of heaven and earth" (14:22). This combination of God's names occurs only here in the Old Testament, although we find similar combinations elsewhere.[9]

Abram may have realized something else. Melchizedek not only worshiped the same God, but also may have been sent by Yahweh at that moment to reaffirm his promise. Earlier, God had told Abram he would "bless those who bless you" (12:3); here, quite unexpectedly and for the first time, someone blessed the patriarch. In this way, the pioneer of our faith received a glimpse into the role of an intercessor, one who represents God to humans and humans to God.

Although the arrival of the king of Sodom was mentioned first, the narrator turned away from him to dwell on Abram's encounter with Melchizedek (14:18–20). Now we return to the conversation between Abram and Sodom's ruler (14:21–24). This king brought Abram no gift but an offer. His offer was abrupt and brief, only six words in Hebrew: Abram should give him the people, but Abram could keep the spoils. This sounds generous. What the king offered would have made Abram much richer than he was. Ironically, Lot had chosen to live near Sodom for material reasons, but lost everything. Abram had trusted God and now stood to gain all of Sodom's wealth, including all of Lot's wealth. The king's offer would also have provided a measure of covenant loyalty between Abram and Sodom. In a dangerous world, such a covenant would have meant added security.

Yet in the king's brusque offer, there is neither gratitude nor generosity, only tight-fisted resentment. Melchizedek brought food and a spoken blessing and was blessed in return. The king of Sodom made a grudging offer and was never mentioned again. Very soon he and his city would be destroyed. Whenever the Old or New Testament writers mentioned Sodom, the context is always bad. By contrast, Melchizedek lodges in the minds of both the ancient Israelites and Christians as an example of the ideal.

This offer by the king of Sodom posed an even greater challenge than the danger Abram had faced by confronting the northern coalition.

Would he choose the tangible reward—money in the bank offered by the king of Sodom—or would he consider Melchizedek's spoken blessing "as good as gold"?[10] International conflicts had been raging, but the consequences of Abram's decision at this moment would be even more far-reaching. In the words of Derek Kidner, "Such a climax shows what was truly at stake in this chapter of international events. The struggle of kings, the far-ranging armies and the spoil of a city are the small-change of the story; the crux is the faith or failure of one man."[11]

Standing in the Valley of Shaveh, Abram's faith was tested. Which would he value more: the immediate gratification of Sodom's wealth that was his by right of recovery, or the spoken blessing of Melchizedek, mere words from a newly discovered compatriot? Abram refused the king's offer. It appears he had made up his mind to do so even before this meeting, for he spoke of having already raised his hand in oath (14:22). He would not take anything from the king of Sodom, "not even a thread or the strap of a sandal" (14:23).

Abram refused to allow the king to take credit for making Abram wealthy (14:23). By doing so he was not just being polite; he was keeping his hands clean. He knew the Sodomites were wicked. And unlike Lot, who had chosen to move closer to Sodom, Abram abstained from anything Sodomite. He wanted to make clear that he was not allied with the king of Sodom. He embarked on this military venture for Lot's sake, not out of any treaty obligation. Abram may also have been sensitive about the source of his wealth. He prospered earlier at Pharaoh's expense, but he did so because of his own poor choices. Refusing the king's offer may have been an expression of Abram's resolve to have only one revenue stream: God. Abram's refusal demonstrated his trust in God's provision and protection as the "Creator of heaven and earth" (14:22). Abram's

ABRAHAM: FATHER OF ALL WHO BELIEVE

refusal to claim the spoils came with two exceptions in order to provide for his allies (14:24). The decision to refuse the king of Sodom
was Abram's and Abram's alone.

In the first part of Genesis 14, we noted Abram's admirable qualities of courage and loyalty. His encounter with the king of Sodom
displayed further admirable qualities: a lack of greed and a desire
to remain unsullied. Most prominent throughout this chapter, however, is Abram's faith. It took great faith in God's protection for
Abram to immediately pursue the powerful northern coalition and
engage them in battle. He trusted God for victory over superior
forces.

Not all crises look the same. Some take the shape of powerful
enemies and overwhelming odds. Others arise from new information that suddenly calls into question what we have understood to
be true. This was the crisis Abram faced in his encounter with
Melchizedek. Abram was following Yahweh, unaware of any others
who worshiped this God. In the valley outside Salem, Abram
became aware of at least one other who worshiped the same God,
but by a different name. If there was one, there might be many more.
Abram was not alone. He had been called to something bigger than
what he understood. The God he served was working in ways
unknown to Abram.

Father Abram is our archetype, for his discovery is one all believers
must embrace. Those who walk by faith must be willing to grow in
their faith. God will not be confined to our understanding of him.
He insists on being released from the boxes in which we would con-
fine him. We express our faith through our stated beliefs, but our faith
is not in our doctrines. Our faith is in the One who has revealed himself to us in Scripture. He will never reveal himself in opposition to
what we find there, but he delights in exploding our preconceptions,
as he did when Abram met Melchizedek.

70

Melchizedek's appearance revealed something else about God's redemptive plan. The plan was bigger than Abram understood it to be, and it involved humans carrying out their orders. Abram already knew this, since God's plan included his own obedience. What he learned from Melchizedek was God's intention to provide an intermediary, a priest, to represent God to the people and the people to God. Perhaps this encounter helped Abram better understand the priestly nature of his own role: "All peoples on earth will be blessed through you" (12:3). Whether Abram understood all of this or not, his descendants certainly did, embracing Melchizedek as a symbol of the perfect intermediary. When the author of Hebrews described Melchizedek as a type of Christ, he was only unfolding the implications latent in this startling scene outside Salem.

Abram set an example of faith in his willingness to put greater trust in the unseen certainty of Melchizedek's blessing than in tangible treasure from Sodom. Abram believed the Creator of heaven and earth was a more reliable source of reward than any king could be. Because this was not an easy choice, God helped Abram. He expanded Abram's household so he could field his own militia; he gave that militia victory over a powerful enemy; and he introduced Abram to Melchizedek. Of course, Abram could have missed all these helps, assuming prosperity and victory were his own doing and resisting the truth that God had others on his team. It was by faith that Abram interpreted these circumstances as divine blessing rather than coincidence.

Abram helped himself in yet another way. He did not wait until the moment of decision to make up his mind. He anticipated what was coming and arrived at a firm decision as to his direction long before the king of Sodom made his offer. The best decisions are those made before the moment of crisis, because these decisions emerge from our deepest loyalties rather than out of surprise or miscalculation.

Abram's deepest loyalty was to Yahweh in spite of temptations to the contrary. One such temptation arose from the difficult circumstances in which Abram found himself. It could not have been easy for the elderly Abram to marshal a militia and march many miles to battle a coalition of kingdoms. Nor would any of this have been necessary if Lot had chosen to remain closer to the center of Canaan and thereby avoid the territory around Sodom. Challenging circumstances can test our loyalty to God by tempting us to despair. Ours is a world torn by conflict and warfare, often involving situations even more dire than those Abram faced. Our world is sullied by sinfulness, not unlike the wickedness of Sodom. A sinful world marred by alienation is not easy to inhabit because it tempts us to give up hope that things can get better. Abram's faith enabled him to remain loyal to God in spite of the difficulties. God has promised to remove the curse of sin from this world. This redemptive act will restore our capacity to be at peace with each other, ourselves, the natural world, and God. If we believe God will keep this promise, we will remain loyal to him no matter what happens in our world.

Another temptation Abram faced was his loyalty to Lot, his own kinsman. Abram expressed his loyalty to Lot by rescuing him and his family from the northern coalition, but Abram's loyalty to his nephew had a limit. Even after this disaster and Abram's rebuff of Sodom's king, Lot did not leave Sodom and move closer to his uncle. Abram must have seen in Lot's decisions dangerous signs of the further weakening of his nephew's moral character. Perhaps Abram's loyalty to Lot tempted him to relocate closer to Sodom in an effort to reclaim his drifting kinsman. If so, Abram resisted this temptation. He would follow Yahweh whether Lot did so or not. However, Abram was not unconcerned about his nephew. In fact, we will soon see him bargaining with Yahweh for Lot's safety.

CONCLUSION

Genesis 14 closes with Abram, the father of the faithful, expressing his firm resolve to trust in God for his blessing and security rather than in humans. In so doing, he left himself temporarily vulnerable and exposed. The next chapter of Genesis opens with a divine message to Abram, one that clearly responds to Abram's faith, yet calls for even greater trust.

A Remarkable Conversation

GENESIS 15

Genesis 15 presents a defining moment in Abram's relationship with God. It opens with God initiating a conversation that results in a powerful demonstration of God's commitment. The narrator arranged the events of this chapter in two parallel scenes. Both scenes open with a divine statement followed by a question from Abram that God answered with both a promise and an object lesson.

GOD'S PROMISE: PART 1 (GEN. 15:1–6)

Genesis 15 opens with God addressing Abram by name for the first time. It is also the first and only time we read of Abram having a vision (15:1). One commentator believes the entire chapter depicts a vision, arguing that this was God's way of showing Abram that their relationship was a "purely spiritual relation of a living fellowship."[1] It is certainly possible that Abram could have experienced a prolonged trance during which these events occurred only in his imagination rather than over the several days it would have taken them to unfold in real time. However, there is nothing trancelike about this or any of God's other appearances to Abram. In each (chs. 15, 17, 18), God showed up in Abram's physical world, once actually stopping by for lunch (18:1). In these chapters, God appears not as an illusion, but in real time and spaced, a preview of the incarnation.

As usual, the narrator spared the details about the setting and timing of these events. We do not know how much time elapsed between these events and those of Genesis 14, only that this encounter took place "after this" (15:1). What the narrator did make clear is that what happened in Genesis 15 happened because of what Abram did in chapter 14.

In the closing verses of the earlier chapter, Abram refused the reward offered by the king of Sodom. He was leery of how accepting the reward might compromise his faithfulness to Yahweh (14:22–24). Genesis 15 opens with God promising Abram a great reward. Some translations speak of God giving Abram this reward, while others speak of God himself being the great reward. By either rendering, God clearly responded to Abram's willingness to deny himself the riches of Sodom in order to remain true to Yahweh. What is more, God promised the blessing pronounced by Melchizedek in Genesis 14:19. God's response anticipated Jesus' words: "Seek first [God's] kingdom and [God's] righteousness, and all these things will be given to you as well" (Matt. 6:33).

We see the connection between the ending of Genesis 14 and the opening of chapter 15 in yet another way. Melchizedek had described God as the one who "delivered" Abram from his enemies (14:20). God chose a nearly identical Hebrew word when he described himself as Abram's "shield" or sovereign (15:1). In the original language, the words *delivered* and *shield* are so close to each other both in sound and proximity that the narrator must have intended for us to see the connection. God had protected and would continue to watch over his friend. By speaking of both shield and reward, God showed his intention to provide Abram with everything he needed: protection from harm and abundant supply.

Much about God's opening words demonstrates God's mercy in revealing himself to a lowly, finite human. Perhaps this is why Abram's response strikes us as inappropriate, even insolent. God stooped to promise to be everything Abram needed, and Abram complained.

Abram felt free to complain not in spite of God's mercy, but precisely because of it. Abram recognized that God had taken the relationship to a new level of familiarity and privilege. God invited honesty, and Abram took that invitation seriously. This clearly illustrates the faith for which Abram would later be commended.

Abram's faith is seen both in the confidence with which he questioned God and in the term used to refer to him: *Adonai Yahweh* (15:2). Whether rendered as "Sovereign LORD" or "Lord GOD" (NRSV), this term clarifies Abram's ultimate trust in God's control. Abram's faith can also be seen in the content of his question. He believed God could make him very wealthy, but he questioned whether any amount of riches could erase the shame of childlessness. Being unable to produce a child represented what one commentator called an "unmitigated disaster in the ancient world."[2] "I remain childless" (15:2) could be translated more literally as "I am walking stripped." Even with the great wealth Abram already had, he felt naked without a child of his own.

To drive his point home, Abram emphasized his lack of a biological son by referring to his servant and heir as the "heir of my house" (15:2 NRSV). He seemed to be saying, "I don't have a real son, so I'm stuck having to make a son out of my servant." Abram also mentioned his servant's name, although this wasn't strictly necessary. Perhaps Abram was making the subtle point that his heir would be Eliezer, a name meaning "God is help" as a way to appeal for God's help in giving Abram a son. Abram added the words "to me" in verse 3 (NASB) as if to say, "I'm supposed to be favored by you, but you still haven't given me a son of my own."

In response to Abram's respectful but pointed challenge, God offered both a thrilling promise and an object lesson to drive the promise home. God connected his response in verse 4 to Abram's assertion in verse 3; the same Hebrew participle appears at the beginning of both statements. God had already promised Abram an heir, but this time God made it clear that this heir would come from Abram's own body. God even used the same term, *seed* (15:5), that Abram had employed in his complaint (15:3).

God took Abram outside the tent in which they had been conversing and directed his attention to the starlit sky. Scientists tell us we can see anywhere from 2,500 to 5,000 stars with the naked eye under ideal conditions. Since Abram's descendants would eventually number in the millions, God's point was not to equate the number of visible stars with the actual number of Abram's eventual offspring. In fact, there are many, many more stars that we cannot see, which may be why God added the phrase, "If indeed you can count them" (15:5). Beyond pointing out the obvious fact that Abram could not count all the stars, this phrase may have been God's way of saying that he saw what Abram could not. One reason we cannot see all the stars is that the earth blocks our view. God may have been reminding Abram (and us) that God's omnipresence gives him an unobstructed view of everything. This nighttime object lesson reinforced God's promise to Abram and gave him something to hold on to in the years of waiting that would follow.

Even in this chapter, which contains so many remarkable events, Abram's response stands out: "Abram believed the LORD" (15:6). The narrator tipped us off to the importance of this response by doing something he rarely did. He inserted an evaluative judgment about Abram's actions: "And [Yahweh] credited it to him as righteousness" (15:6). In Abram's response, we find the first appearance of the verb *believe* in the Old Testament. However impossible it seemed that God could bring forth an heir from Abram's aged body, he believed this is exactly what would happen.

In response to Abram's remarkable faith, God credited it to him as righteousness. Although only three words in Hebrew, this phrase has deep implications. At its simplest level, it indicates that God was pleased with Abram's response. On a deeper level, this phrase reveals God's pleasure and the deciding characteristic of Abram's descendants: They are people of faith.

The apostle Paul noted an even deeper significance to this phrase, one that had become clear since the coming of Christ. The phrase became a motto not only for Abram's physical descendants, but also for all who desire to be reconciled to God. The writer of Hebrews made this point negatively: "Without faith it is impossible to please God" (Heb. 11:6). Paul stated the same point positively: "To the one who does not work but trusts God who justifies the ungodly, their faith is credited as righteousness" (Rom. 4:5), whether Jew or Gentile. As one commentator expressed it, "While Genesis implies that the sons of Abram must be men of faith, Paul turns the words around and explains, 'it is men of faith who are the sons of Abraham' (Gal. 3:7)."[3] Perhaps at no other point is Abram's role as archetype more clearly seen. He demonstrated the secret to becoming God's friend: faith.

GOD'S PROMISE: PART 2 (GEN. 15:7–21)

Abram's believing response to the promises in scene one (15:6) leads into scene two (15:7–21). In fact, Abram's response in scene one is the reason scene two happens at all. Faith is like a ladder; success at one rung provides access to the next.

Scene two begins as scene one did, with a divine statement concerning God's relationship with Abram: "I am the LORD, who brought you out of Ur of the Chaldeans to give you this land to take possession of it" (15:7). When God first promised the land, it was to Abram's offspring (12:7). One chapter later, God repeated this promise, but Abram received two promises of land (13:15–17).

Chapter 15 contains the fourth promise of the land and the third time God specifically promised it to Abram himself. Why did Abram choose this time to respond with a question? Perhaps because of what had taken place in Genesis 14. There Abram experienced conflict with invading armies and stubborn inhabitants, apparently insurmountable obstacles to God's promise that the land would belong to him. Perhaps those obstacles made it easier to believe that God would give the land to Abram's descendants rather than directly to himself. Note the personal focus of his question in 15:8: "Sovereign LORD, how can I know that I will gain possession of it?"

Once again, Abram's question was not a sign of disbelief but evidence of faith. He knew God was sovereign and that he stood in a right relationship with this God. He also knew that Yahweh was willing to provide tangible assurances; he had already shown Abram the dust on the ground (13:16) and the stars in the sky (15:5). The earlier object lessons strengthened his faith to ask for yet another tangible assurance. That Abram wanted something tangible can be seen in how he began his question: "How can I know that . . ." (15:8). Faith exercised fosters greater faith.

God did not disappoint Abram. On the contrary, he responded by providing one of the most incredible object lessons found in the Old Testament (15:9–17). The ceremony that followed gave the tangible assurance Abram sought and clarified his role. It revealed the future of his descendants and illustrated the culmination of the redemptive plan.

In response to Abram's question, God issued a series of commands. Abram was to take from his flocks and herds specific animals of a certain age and bring them to God, presumably to the place God designated. God either instructed Abram to cut the larger animals in half lengthwise and lay them opposite one another, or else Abram figured out what God intended to do and prepared the animals accordingly. Abram realized this would be a covenant-making ceremony, known around the ancient Near East as a way of commemorating contractual arrangements. More precisely, this would be something like a royal land-grant treaty, through which a king awarded territory to a loyal subject. The animals would be laid out on the ground and someone would walk between the pieces as if to say, "May what happened to these animals happen to me if I break this deal."

Although no altar was present, sacrifice was central to this ceremony. The animals included were the very animals the Israelites would later sacrifice to Yahweh and represented the Israelites who would descend from Abram. The three-year-old heifer, goat, and ram likely represented the three generations that would elapse before the fourth generation returned to Canaan (see 15:16).

Then Abram waited for a while. Scavenger birds have poor eyesight and depend on their sense of smell to discover rotting carcasses. Abram had to wait so long that the animals started to stink, perhaps to remind him and us that God's promises are not fulfilled immediately. The vultures may also have represented those people and forces that would oppose Abram and his descendants. Vultures are appropriate symbols, being birds that feed on what is dead. After all, the aged Abram was as good as dead in regard to his ability to father many nations. It was as if the rotting smell of unfulfilled promises drew the buzzards. This is why it is so significant that Abram drove away the birds. He believed God would act, even when all of his senses told him all hope was gone.

The sun was setting, and it grew darker. Abram started to fall asleep, not a natural slumber but a deep sleep, more like what happened to Adam in the garden of Eden (see 2:21). Then a darkness deeper than any starless night crept over the slumbering Abram. The combination of natural darkness, the darkness of sleep, and this supernatural blackness may represent the bleak situation the Israelites later faced as they descended into Egyptian slavery.

Finally, at this blackest point, God revealed himself. The revelation he made in the dark surpassed any previous message he had brought to Abram. Out of the darkness he began, "Know for certain" (15:13), a Hebrew phrase that made the following statement more emphatic. God's message concerned Abram's descendants. For the first time, Abram learned that these descendants would be strangers in a foreign country where they would be enslaved and mistreated for four hundred years. But then God would punish the enslaving nation and bring out the captives with great wealth (15:13–14).

As for Abram, God promised he would die at a "good old age" and receive proper burial (15:15). While Abram would not live to see the culmination of God's plan, he would experience what everyone in that day would consider a great blessing, a peaceful death and respectful burial after a long and full life. In those days, burial was not just a way to dispose of a dead body. It was a way for a loving family to honor the life of the deceased. A good ending to Abram's life is summed up in the word *shalom* (peace), used here for the first time in Scripture (15:15).

But the story would not end at Abram's death. His descendants would return in the fourth generation (15:16), another way of referring to the four hundred years mentioned above, and a round number for 430, the actual number of years Abram's descendants would spend in slavery in Egypt (Ex. 12:40). The reason for this apparent delay in God's plan was that the sins of the current inhabitants of Canaan, known here as the Amorites (although several other nationalities were also in residence), had "not yet reached its full measure" (Gen. 15:16).

Why did God tell all this to Abram? It couldn't have been encouraging for him to hear of the future enslavement of his descendants, along with the fact that he would be long dead when God's promises would finally be fulfilled. God seemed to have had several reasons for providing this information. First, it was appropriate that Abram, the pioneer of God's redemptive plan, should learn how the next several centuries of this plan would proceed. Second, God wanted Abram and his descendants to understand that delay was part of God's design. He would allow time to elapse between the issuing of his promises and their fulfillment. Abram had already experienced such a delay; his offspring would as well.

Delay is not denial. God was not saying "no" but "wait." Delay is not a sign of God's weakness but of his wisdom. Knowing that the right thing at the wrong time is the wrong thing, God would wait until the time was right. In his wisdom, he knew it would be best to bring about the punishment of the Amorites through the arrival of the Israelites. Wise delay takes patience, as the apostle Peter understood when he wrote, "The Lord is not slow in keeping his promise, as some understand slowness. Instead he is patient with you, not wanting anyone to perish, but everyone to come to repentance" (2 Pet. 3:9).

A third reason God may have had for revealing the future to Abram was to demonstrate his desire for reconciliation, even with the disobedient Amorites. After all, he had placed his servants among them; we know only of Melchizedek and Abram, but there might have been others faithfully testifying to their Canaanite neighbors of the one true God. This revelation of God's patient delay may have been what inspired Abram to later appeal to God's fairness on behalf of the cities of Sodom and Gomorrah for the sake of any righteous people who might reside there (Gen. 18).

Fourth, God's revelation to Abram showed the patriarch and his offspring that their God was righteous and, though he preferred to be merciful, punishment would come to those who rejected his appeals.

A fifth reason God related this information to Abram may have been to make clear that God is eternal. Time is never an enemy of God, only a tool employed for his purposes. Knowing the events of the succeeding centuries, Abram and his descendants would understand that God is always capable of keeping his word, even in the case of delay. This episode may have been in Abraham's mind when he named Yahweh "the Eternal God" (21:33). Perhaps this lesson kept the coals of memory smoldering in Abram's descendants through the centuries of their slavery in Egypt until Moses arrived to fan them into the flame of faith.

Sixth, God may have informed Abram of what was to come so he and the Israelites would understand how committed in love he was to his people—a promise-keeping God. He would keep his promise to give the land to the Israelites and to Abram through the Israelites. He would also keep his promise to bless those who blessed Abram's descendants and punish those who mistreated them. This appears to be the reason God specified that the Israelites would "come out with great possessions" (15:14), rich compensation for their forced labor. He would keep his promises, even if centuries elapsed between the making and keeping of them.

As it was with the archetype of our salvation, so it is with his spiritual offspring: Those who follow God must walk by faith. If divine promises were always immediately fulfilled and delay was never part of God's plan, faith would be unnecessary. But since God almost always allows for delay between the making and keeping of promises, faith is essential. As the writer to the Hebrews reminds us, "Without faith it is impossible to please God, because anyone who comes to him must believe . . . that he rewards those who earnestly seek him" (Heb. 11:6).

Nothing in Abram's story—indeed, nothing in the Bible to this point—prepares us for what happened next. God waited for the blackest moment of this encounter to give Abram the clearest demonstration of his divine nature. As Abram watched, two familiar objects appeared: a smoking firepot and a blazing torch (Gen. 15:17). Nomads were accustomed to using the former as a way of transporting fire from one campsite to the next. The coals from the previous night's fire were kept smoldering until the travelers reached the next stopping place where the embers would be used to start that night's fire. Torches functioned like flashlights or street lights, making it possible to move around after dark. Both items were essential for ancients, especially those on the move. By causing them to appear here, God may have been saying that his people were to be pilgrims in need of the light of God's guidance.

The torch and the firepot produce different effects. A torch illumines, but a firepot obscures vision with its billowing smoke. One reveals and the other conceals. In this they symbolize a God who conceals himself even as he reveals himself. Centuries later, Mount Sinai, where God clearly revealed his will for the Israelites, was engulfed in smoke and fire while the Israelites camped there. Even in the incarnation, his true nature was hidden from sight, so that "the world did not recognize him" (John 1:10). Abram and his descendants needed to understand that though God had made himself known to them, they could not fully know him, for "the secret things belong to the LORD our God" (Deut. 29:29).

Even more incredible than the appearance of these objects that symbolized God's presence is what they did once they appeared. They passed between the animal pieces. By doing this, God committed himself to keeping the promises he had made; his eternal nature is the guarantee. God promises to keep his word or else cease to be God. The world would not see a comparable example of God accommodating himself to humanity until he incarnated himself in Jesus. In this encounter with Abram, God promised to surrender his life rather than break his promise. In Christ, God gave up his life to fulfill his promised redemption.

The closing verses of Genesis 15 summarize God's promise to give the land of Canaan, which was then occupied by many nations, to Abram's offspring (15:18–21). By adding this summary, the narrator emphasized the certainty that from Abram will come "descendants"; the same term used in verses 3, 5, and 13. The extensive boundaries described suggest there will be lots of room, implying lots of descendants. Because the current inhabitants of the land are specifically mentioned, we understand the impossibility of obtaining this land without God's help.

CONCLUSION

Abram is our father in faith. He is the archetype of our faith. His experience with God served as a paradigm for what all believers experience. He also provided an example for how to walk by faith. He was the pioneer of God's redemptive plan, the next several centuries of which are revealed in Genesis 15:12–18. This plan developed slowly with periods of delay. It involved difficulties, such as slavery in Egypt. Even to the pioneer of this plan, God revealed its details only partly. To take part in such a plan takes faith. Only faith enables us to turn away from security and embrace insecurity, exchanging the known for the unknown. Only by faith can we accept what is impossible as not only possible, but certain. Only through faith can we endure delay and difficulties and only the one who trusts is content to know in part.

God honors this faith. "Abram believed the LORD, and he credited it to him as righteousness" (15:6). Faith is always the right response when God speaks. The apostle Paul considered the words "it was credited to him" to be not only for Abram, "but also for us, to whom God will credit righteousness—for us who believe in him who raised Jesus our Lord from the dead" (Rom. 4:24).

In Abram's experience in Egypt, we witnessed how stumbling doubt often follows moments of great faith. The next chapter will provide another sad example of failure, but also a bright picture of God's faithfulness despite the lack of Abram's faith.

6

Coming to God's Rescue

It would be surprising to see how quickly Abram moves from a shining moment of faith to yet another blundering episode if this tendency were not so familiar in our own lives. In Genesis 15, the sovereign God stooped to Abram's weakness and revealed his plan and character in unprecedented ways. Yet Genesis 16 shows that Abram and Sarai felt they needed to give God a helping hand. Actually, Abram played only a minor role in these events, but neither he nor Sarai appear in a positive light. The real hero of this story, as with all stories in the Bible, is God. His actions in dealing with Hagar provide rich insights into his character and redemptive plan.

SARAI'S PLAN (GEN. 16:1–6)

By mentioning Sarai's barrenness in the opening verse of this chapter, the narrator drew us back to the divine promise spoken to

Abram a few verses earlier: "A son who is your own flesh and blood will be your heir" (15:4). We can almost hear Sarai's thoughts: "If Abram is to physically father a son, that son will have to come through another woman. What about Hagar, my servant girl?"

We are repelled by the idea of a wife encouraging her husband to sleep with another woman, but this was entirely acceptable in the culture of the ancient world. Hagar was not just any woman but Sarai's slave, therefore her property. For a time, God permitted this and other practices (for example, polygamy and slavery), though he would eventually lead his people toward a better way. Wherever God has worked, he has taken the culture largely as he found it, knowing this made it easier for people of that culture to understand and follow him. He established a different way where necessary (for example, the absolute rejection of idolatry), but generally accommodated himself to a culture before transforming it by transforming its people.

Sarai certainly understood that adding a second wife would make the household much more complicated, but what could she do? The path to experiencing God's promised blessings passed through her womb, and that womb was shut tight.

She did not make any secret about the cause of her barrenness. It was caused by Yahweh himself, the same God who had made the promises. She said, "The LORD has kept me from having children" (16:2). We do not know whether Sarai made her statement about Yahweh in a matter-of-fact way or with a hint of frustration. In either case, her statement put the problem at God's doorstep, where it belonged.

People in the ancient world tended to emphasize the role of God or the gods in life's events. If this scenario were played out today, we would likely point to the more immediate cause for Sarai's barrenness, such as some physical or medical problem. Ultimately, however, the inability to bear children results from sin; not the sin of the barren woman or her husband, but the sin that has diseased our world. God's purpose in calling Abram was to begin the plan that would rid the world of sin's curse. He may have been the pioneer of this redemptive plan, but sin's effects were still deeply felt in Abram's own family.

We cannot be sure what Abram was thinking at this time. If he believed God would miraculously open Sarai's womb, he left us no clue. All God had told him up to this point was that he would physically father an heir. Later, God made it clear that Sarai would be the mother of that child (17:16), but that information was unknown to Abram at this point. Since God could have revealed this part of the plan any time he wished, we assume he had a reason for keeping this couple in the dark. As difficult as things would be for all involved, God had his reasons for allowing what happened next, the birth of Ishmael.

Abram agreed to Sarai's plan to conceive a child through Hagar. No mention is made of Abram asking for God's will in the matter. Nor is there any mention of anyone asking Hagar's opinion. In that culture, the opinion of a slave was unimportant. Besides, Hagar would likely have welcomed this opportunity to advance her position from that of a slave to a second wife.

What was wrong with Sarai's plan? Given what the couple knew, Sarai seemed justified in proposing this course of action. The method she suggested was legitimate by the standards of the ancient Near East, an early version of surrogacy.

While Sarai's strategy was understandable and legal, the narrator made clear that it was also flawed. We see this in several ways. First, through hindsight we recognize that, although God loved Ishmael and allowed him to be born, he was not God's choice for the heir. Ishmael's presence in the family caused a great deal of pain for all involved. Second, if Sarai's motives were pure, she would not have reacted harshly when Hagar became pregnant.

Also, the narrator expressed his disapproval in a more subtle way by describing the scenario in terms that remind us of Adam and Eve in Genesis 3. In both instances, a wife took the initiative in doing something contrary to God's will, and the husband obeyed. Note how the narrator took pains to point out that Sarai was Abram's wife, mentioning it twice (16:1, 3). We already know this, but the repetition provides a stronger link to Genesis 3. The narrator also used the same phrase for "agreed" (16:2) that he had used to describe Adam's actions (3:17). In both stories, the wife gave something to the husband that he accepted, and in both cases, the outcome was disastrous. The point is not that men should never listen to their wives, but that God's plan may require us to wait for him in faith, even against the advice of those closest to us.

The narrator also emphasized Hagar's nationality. Presumably, she joined Abram's household during the ill-advised visit to Egypt. She may even have been part of the dowry paid by Pharaoh. Perhaps the narrator was hinting at the questionable wisdom of Sarai's plan by connecting it to a place Abram should never have gone and a deed he should never have done. Although Egypt is not mentioned here as the place where the Israelites would spend centuries of slavery, future readers clearly make this association, thereby tainting the choice to involve Hagar due to her association with Egypt. On the other hand, referring to Hagar's nationality might have hinted at something more hopeful. After all, God's redemptive plan involved reconciling all nations to himself and all peoples to one another. Perhaps allowing an Egyptian slave girl to experience Abram's blessing was God's way of pointing to the ultimate blessings God had in store.

The narrator added that the events described took place after Abram had lived in Canaan for ten years (16:3). This reference to time is the first of two in this chapter (see 16:16). Because such temporal references are scarce in this narrative, these are significant. Ten years earlier God had promised an elderly couple that they would have a host of offspring who would possess this land. Now any possibility that Sarai might conceive had faded from remote to nonexistent. Abram's household had grown in those ten years, but the possibility of Abram's family possessing the land must also have seemed even more unlikely. Time was running out, something had to be done, and it looked like it was up to Abram and Sarai to do it.

Abram had sexual intercourse with his new wife, and she conceived. It took some time for Hagar to realize she was pregnant, but the narrator made it seem instantaneous. Abram and Sarai had been trying to conceive for so long without success that they had given up hope. Now, seemingly in an instant, a child was on the way.

Hagar must have been thrilled at becoming pregnant so quickly. This child would ensure her important status in the household. Abram, too, would have been delighted with the news. Finally, God's plan was coming to pass. For Sarai, however, the whole thing was galling. What she had failed to do for decades, Hagar had accomplished immediately. Even worse, the whole thing had been Sarai's idea. The very sight of a pregnant Hagar must have been hard for Sarai to take. Most annoying of all was Hagar's new attitude. Whereas before she had shown respect for her mistress, she now treated Sarai with disdain. Once Sarai's slave, Hagar now acted as her superior.

Sarai took out her frustration not on Hagar, but on Abram. He was, after all, now responsible for Hagar. "My violence upon you," she sputtered (Gen. 16:5, paraphrase). *Violence* seems like a strong word to describe what Hagar had begun to do. "It was I who put my slave-girl into your arms but, now she knows that she has conceived, I count for nothing in her eyes" (16:5 NJB). It was as if she were saying to Abram, "This may have been my idea, but how dare you allow things to get out of hand like this." Abram could have tried to

ABRAHAM: FATHER OF ALL WHO BELIEVE

placate Sarai or he could have spoken to Hagar about her treatment of Sarai. Instead he washed his hands of Hagar and returned her to Sarai (16:6). The child would still be his heir, but Hagar would be Sarai's responsibility.

Sarai wasted no time in making life miserable for Hagar. The word used to describe her treatment of Hagar was used in the preceding chapter to describe how the Egyptians would later treat the Israelites (15:13; compare Ex. 1:11–12; Deut. 26:6). When Hagar could stand it no longer, she ran away.

The events of Genesis 16 thus far do not reflect well on either Abram or Sarai. He married a second wife, whom he allowed to be abused to the point that she ran away, taking his heir with her. In all this, he appeared weak and fearful. Sarai had concocted an idea to help along God's plan, but then she abandoned both her idea and the lives of two other human beings when things did not work out as she had intended. Both Abram and Sarai were guilty of folding under the pressure of divine delay. Earlier we noted how sin corrupts the natural world, producing barrenness. This scene also demonstrates how sin corrupts human society by turning people against each other and prompting shameful behavior toward others. Although Abram is the pioneer of God's redemptive plan, he and his wife both stood in desperate need of its reconciling effects.

HAGAR'S ENCOUNTER WITH THE ANGEL (GEN. 16:7–14)

The first person in the Bible to receive an angelic visit was a runaway slave girl (16:7). The narrator caught the significance of this encounter by stating that "the LORD . . . spoke to her" (16:13). This emphasizes how remarkable it was that God sent an angel to speak to a servant girl while Abram and Sarai heard nothing. Do not miss the implication. Although God loves everyone, he takes special note of the afflicted, the outsiders, the weak, and the "throw-aways." Those who matter little to others, matter much to God.

Once again, God intervened to preserve his plan. He had done this once before, in Egypt, forcing Pharaoh to return Sarai to her husband. Now God confronted another Egyptian, directing her to return to Sarai, her mistress. As we saw earlier, if Sarai had remained in Egypt, Abram would have been forced to abandon either his wife or his plan. Here, if God had not stopped Hagar from running away, Abram would have lost his son and possibly his hope that the plan could ever be realized.

The angel encountered Hagar in the Negev between Kadesh and Bered (16:14), near a spring in the desert (16:7). She had been head-ing south, probably trying to get back to Egypt. Use of the verb *found* suggests the angel had gone looking for her. That he knew her name implies he already knew about her situation. These facts make his two questions all the more striking: "Where have you come from, and where are you going?" (16:8). Since the angel already knew the answers, the questions must have been for her ben-efit. This encounter was Hagar's opportunity to understand her role in God's plan.

Note how the angel referred to her. He called her "Hagar, slave-girl of Sarai" (16:8 NRSV). He addressed her not as Abram's wife or as the mother of Abram's heir, but as Sarai's slave. His message to her was that she should return to her mistress and submit to her. Her plan to run back to Egypt would not work. She must go back in Abram's household where her son could grow up with protection and provision.

The son's name, Ishmael, meaning "God hears," would preserve the memory of this encounter between the Sovereign of the universe and a runaway foreign slave girl; every mention of his name would bring a reminder that God does indeed listen. Ishmael would become the ancestor of many, many descendants (16:10). The fulfillment of this promise is evident in the long list of peoples who trace their lineage back to Ishmael (25:12–18).

The description of Ishmael in 16:12 sounds less promising: "He will be a wild donkey of a man; his hand will be against everyone and everyone's hand against him." Yet perhaps this was not bad news at all. Since the biblical material is generally favorable to or neutral about Ishmael and his descendants, we should be hesitant to see this as the prediction of something negative. Just as a wild donkey is free and unbridled, this son of a slave woman would not be a servant to anyone. The last part of the verse likely predicts a nomadic existence. That these two lifestyles — nomadic and sedentary — are often in conflict with each other explains the mention of animosity. Or perhaps we should see this in terms of "otherness" rather than conflict, as in, "He shall dwell over against all his kinsmen" (16:12 ESV). The knowledge that her son would live as a free man and be the father of many nations must have been welcome news to Hagar, the slavegirl.

This son would not, however, be Abram's promised heir. He would be blessed because he was Abram's son, but he would not be the child promised in Genesis 15:4. That child would be the ancestor of another group of people that would inhabit the land of Canaan. Ishmael's destiny lay elsewhere, like a wild donkey, away from settled populations. Hagar's child, while blessed, would not be the child of promise.

Hagar's response is impressive. She had already admitted to her place as Sarai's servant girl, not Abram's wife, and that she was running away from her mistress (16:8). She voiced no complaint about having to return to a life of slavery. She understood that in exchange for her freedom, her son would receive the blessings of being Abram's son.

Hagar knew she had encountered Yahweh himself (16:13), and she was captivated by the realization that God had noticed her. She gave a name to God, and was the first person in the Bible to do so. She called him *El Roi*, "the God who sees." Her added explanatory phrase might be a question: "Have I truly seen the One who sees me?" (16:13 NLT) or a statement: "I have now seen the One who sees me" (NIV), but it seems more likely a statement of wonder: "Have I even remained alive here after seeing Him?" (NASB). Whichever way we understand Hagar's words, they express delight and amazement that God would appear to someone like her. This is the only place in Scripture where this name is used for God, but the name stuck with the well (16:14), which continued to play a part in the lives of the patriarchs (see 24:62; 25:11).

ISHMAEL'S BIRTH (GEN. 16:15–16)

Hagar returned to the household of Abram, where she gave birth to her son. Upon her return, Abram appeared to be protecting her in a way he had not earlier. Now when Sarai complained about Hagar and Ishmael, she had to take her complaints to Abram rather than deal with Hagar herself (21:10). The narrator specifically mentioned that it was Abram who named Ishmael (16:15), implying that Abram "adopted" him as his son. We do not know how much Hagar told Abram about what the angel had promised concerning their child. She must have told him what their son was to be named, but did she tell him everything else? Likely not. Abram seemed to have considered Ishmael the promised heir, but God would clear up that misconception thirteen years later (see 17:20–21).

The narrator informed us that the birth and naming of Ishmael took place when Abram was eighty-six years old (16:16). Perhaps his comment is intended to draw attention to the remarkable, though not impossible, fact that a man this age was able to father a child so quickly. More likely, mentioning Abram's age is a reminder that eleven years have elapsed since God first called Abram and promised him vast numbers of descendants.

Genesis 16 does not exhibit the father of believers at the top of his game. The faith he demonstrated in Genesis 15 did not help him withstand his wife's suggestion to father a child with Hagar. Yesterday's faith cannot help with today's challenges. To his credit, Abram showed incredible patience to wait as long as he did. And when Hagar returned, Abram owned up to his mistakes and took responsibility for his choices by adopting Ishmael and protecting Hagar. Abram had learned important lessons through this episode.

As the archetype of our salvation, Abram's lessons shed light on our walk as well. He learned once again of his weakness and need to depend on God, but he also learned about God's patience and willingness to work with him. Further, Abram learned about God's concern for the poor, abused, and marginalized. God hears. To hear that Hagar had seen Yahweh must have made quite an impression on Abram. His Egyptian-born second wife had seen a manifestation of God as many times as he had. This God cannot be contained by any parameters we choose to build around him. If Yahweh wants to appear to a foreign slave girl but not to Abram and Sarai, it is his choice. Abram must trust him and walk by faith. This is how we too must live.

Other lessons in this chapter show the blessings of following God. Abram had finally been granted an heir, this boy whose name was a reminder that God saw what was happening in Abram's family. God had also intervened in the life of Hagar not only because she was in need, but also because of her connection with Abram. It was better for Hagar to be a second wife and slave in Abram's household than free elsewhere. Abram understood that although he might stumble, God would faithfully carry out the plan. Such blessings strengthened Abram's faith in God's covenant promises; they strengthen our faith as well.

God had entered into a covenant with Abram in order to remove the curse of sin; this episode provides ample evidence that such a plan was necessary. We can see the effects of the curse in Sarai's barrenness and in her bitterness. Sin is what enables something as precious as the relationship between a husband and wife to become an opportunity for temptation and stumbling. Only in a cursed world are people held as slaves; only in such a world would one be forced to choose between freedom for oneself and blessings for one's son. The pioneer of this plan was discovering firsthand the need for reconciliation.

Abram was reminded also that while God had a plan, he revealed it only on a need-to-know basis. And it would be God, not Abram, who decided what should be known and when. After God's general promise, Abram heard relatively little from God. Even when Abram made decisions that jeopardized the plan, God remained silent. He withheld information that could have prevented poor choices until after Abram had made a decision.

If you have a supervisory role at work, I do not recommend this approach. Those who report to you probably won't like being kept in the dark. They will feel stifled and unable to exercise their own creative and problem-solving skills. Your supervisors may not like it either, objecting to inefficiencies and wasted expenditures.

If this is not the best way to lead people, why does God employ this strategy? The answer is that he is not interested in making a profit, building a team, or encouraging creative problem solving. He is interested in producing faith in Abram and his "children." Without faith, no amount of creativity or problem-solving skills will matter. Without faith it is impossible to please God, and pleasing God is what humans were created to do. The best way to build faith is to spend time walking in the silent darkness, learning to trust the One with night vision. God knew that if Abram and his offspring could learn to walk by faith, they would understand their total and absolute dependence on him, and how essential it is that they make his will their will. Our walk with God is not about team building but faith building. It is an opportunity to learn what it means to be God's servants.

Jesus sought to instill this awareness in his followers through one of his parables:

> Suppose one of you has a servant plowing or looking after the sheep. Will he say to the servant when he comes in from the field, "Come along now and sit down to eat"? Won't he rather say, "Prepare my supper, get yourself ready and wait on me while I eat and drink; after that you may eat and drink"? Will he thank the servant because he did what he was told to do? So you also, when you have done everything you were told to do, should say, "We are unworthy servants; we have only done our duty." (Luke 17:7–10)

Yes, we are God's children whom he dearly loves, but we cannot experience the true happiness of this privilege unless we learn to live as God's humble and faithful servants. We might complain that God's strategy allows for too many mistakes, too much wasted time, too much heartache. Genesis 16 has provided plenty of all three. In the midst of our pain, we must remember that nothing is wasted with God. He can use our successes, but he can also use our failures. In fact, those failures may be even more useful because they allow us to see God's power as he weaves those failures into the pattern of his plan.

The results of this episode were not all bad. Abram and Sarai learned important lessons; Hagar was safely returned after seeing God; and a beloved son was added to the household. God can use not only our major successes and failures, but also our little victories. These are especially helpful in demonstrating the difference between the good and the best. Ishmael would have been a good choice for the heir, but he was not God's best choice. Later, when God revealed to Abram that it would be Isaac not Ishmael who would inherit the promises, Abram and Sarai realized that their good works cannot measure up to God's gracious best.

This path of gradual revelation is not an easy one. As we have seen before, faith is like a muscle that must be exercised with increasing resistance if it is to grow stronger. God, too, has set himself up for a difficult task. Letting Abram's offspring live wherever they chose would have been easier; having them settle in a land now occupied by ten nations presented a big challenge. Allowing Eliezer or Ishmael to inherit would have been child's play compared to bringing forth a child from an elderly, barren Sarai. Even as God was building his followers' faith, he appeared to be backing himself into a corner. Yet this would all produce something glorious.

It takes faith to see things this way. From our vantage point, divine delay can look like divine neglect. Heavenly silence seems to suggest divine absence, or worse. But our God hears. We may wonder if God really knows what he is doing or whether he has let things get completely out of control. This is precisely when faith is required. We must make a daily decision—hourly, if necessary—to trust him regardless of how things appear. As we choose to walk by faith, our faith grows. Divine delay and absence are hard to bear, but there is no better way for us to develop trust in God. And developing that trust is our most important job. We must learn to rest in the assurance that God hears.

CONCLUSION

Eleven years had passed since God first called Abram and promised him many descendants and great prosperity. The wait was long and the path arduous, but it was all worth it, now that the promised child, Ishmael, had been born. Or so Abram thought. Little did he know that after another thirteen years, God would once again turn Abram's world on its head.

7

A Watershed Moment

GENESIS 17

Another thirteen years passed with no divine messages or visitations. Then one day out of the blue, God spoke. Earlier in Abram's life, God's appearances came in response to something Abram had done: leaving Harran, parting company with Lot, and refusing any reward from the king of Sodom. This divine visitation in Abram's ninety-ninth year appears to have been unprompted.

The narrator carefully crafted this story to balance the one in Genesis 15. Both begin with a similar divine pronouncement, including an "I am" statement. In Genesis 15, Abram was a model of belief, here a model of obedience. In both chapters, God promised a son. From Genesis 15, we learn the boy will be Abram's biological child; in Genesis 17, we learn he will be Sarai's as well. Both chapters contain a promise of the land. In Genesis 15, God provided a historical survey of how and when the land would be occupied, while in Genesis 17, the emphasis is on the land as an "everlasting possession" (17:8). Genesis 15 focused on Abram's descendants; Genesis 17 shines the spotlight on Abram and Sarai with the changing of their names.

Genesis 15–17 present two positive pictures of Abram surrounding one less positive. We observe something similar in Genesis 12–14, where Abram's step of faith in leaving Harran was followed by his misstep in Egypt then by his faithful actions in connection with Lot (chs. 13–14). While we cannot be completely sure of the narrator's reasons for this arrangement, it has the effect of presenting Abram as human yet remarkably trusting, an excellent example for his physical and spiritual offspring.

GOD RENAMED ABRAM (GEN. 17:1–8)

For only the second time on record, God appeared to Abram. This appearance took place thirteen years after the episode with Hagar and twenty-four years after God called him from Harran. The narrator's reference to Abram's age (ninety-nine years) emphasizes the great length of time Abram had waited and sets us up to be amazed at what God was about to promise. God provided no apology or explanation for the delay, only a word of self-identification and two commands ("I am God Almighty; walk before me faithfully and be blameless"), and a promise (17:1–2). This is the first time in the Bible God is referred to as God Almighty—*El Shaddai*. This name often appears in connection with a promise of descendants, so there is irony in its use here because Abram had only one.[1] Manifestations of God's power have been relatively modest, including the rescue from Pharaoh, military victory over the northern coalition, and material blessings. Abram's faith began with divine claims that seemed too grand for the facts on the ground. True believers accept such claims and trust the character of the One making the promise, even against the evidence we see around us.

To "walk before" God means to be loyal to him. The same phrase was used in the ancient Near East to describe loyalty to the king. The added command to be blameless emphasizes the need to be completely obedient in one's actions. Because God was about to reveal the specific terms of his covenant, these two commands spell out Abram's general obligation.

God's promise in 17:2 summarizes his previous assurances to Abram, specifically the assurance of multiplied offspring. God also announced his intention to confirm these promises more formally by making a covenant. If we think of the earlier promises as an engagement, the covenant to be made here is the wedding ceremony in which God would confirm what he had promised.

Abram's response, falling facedown, indicates his complete loyalty to Yahweh, his King. This was the posture one assumed in the presence of ancient Near Eastern royalty. God responded to this gesture of loyalty by spelling out the specific terms of the covenant (17:4–9). First God stated his responsibility, then spelled out Abram's. God's part involved making Abram the "father of many nations" (17:4). Once again God expanded on earlier promises, specifying here that not only would Abram have many descendants, but these descendants would form multiple nations. We learn later that these nations included not only the Israelites, but also the Ishmaelites and Edomites (through Abram's son Ishmael and grandson Esau). Abram's progeny would extend even further, for he was, according to the apostle Paul, the spiritual father of all who believe (Rom. 4:11).

God reaffirmed his promise to Abram and graciously added a confirming element to it. In Genesis 15, God had promised numerous descendants and confirmed that promise by bringing Abram out under the stars. Here the confirmation involved changing Abram's name to Abraham, signifying both his partnership with God and his new status as father of many nations (17:5). The name Abraham does not mean "father of many nations" as is often thought. If that had been God's intended meaning, he would have changed Abram's name to Abhamon. The names Abram and Abraham mean the same thing: "great father." However the second form adds a syllable beginning with the Hebrew letter *hey*. This same letter begins the Hebrew word *hamon*, which means "many nations." So God changed the significance of Abram's name, not its meaning. By lengthening the name, God signified the wider extent of Abraham's blessing. By lengthening the name with the first letter of *hamon*, he signified Abraham's role as "father of many nations."

Each use of Abraham's name, either by himself or another person, would now testify to God's promise to him and his descendants. However, the new name does not tell the whole story. Only those who remembered the divine promise and lived by faith in its fulfillment would know the true significance of Abraham's new name. The only clues were a longer name and the letter *hey*, but to a believer in God these would be sufficient reminders of all he had promised. Those who believed would accept the fact that God was intent on fulfilling his promise in spite of its seeming impossibility.

As before, God restated his promise to Abraham while adding a new element. In addition to asserting that Abraham would be very fruitful, God told the patriarch he would be the father of kings (17:6). That the covenant would be not only for Abraham, but also for his descendants was suggested earlier, and that notion is highlighted here (17:7–8). The phrase, "between me and you and your descendants after you," used six times in Genesis 17, is found in ancient Near Eastern legal documents indicating that property will pass to the next generation without restriction.

For the first time, God defined this covenant as eternal (17:7). Also, in Genesis 15:18, God had described the boundaries and inhabitants of the Promised Land, but here, for the first time, God identified this land as Canaan. Another first is the use of the phrase "and I will be their God" (17:8), used frequently in the Old Testament, often with another phrase, "they will be my people." The use of one or both phrases became shorthand for the covenant God was establishing with Abraham and his descendants.

GOD SET TERMS OF COVENANT: CIRCUMCISION (GEN. 17:9–14)

After stating what he would do, God described the obligations of Abraham and his descendants. Specifying that Abraham and his descendants were obligated to obey implies Abraham's responsibility to pass on these instructions to succeeding generations. This is the first passage in the Old Testament that speaks of preserving and transmitting divine instruction.

Obedience to the covenant was to be registered in a sacred ritual: circumcision for each male child at the age of eight days. Other nations in the ancient world practiced partial circumcision as a puberty or prenuptial act. Israel was to be different in two ways: Circumcision was to be performed on infants and would be complete. The command was addressed to "you" plural (17:10–11), indicating that it included not only Abraham, but also his descendants. Twice we are told that circumcision was to be done to all the males in the household, whether descended from Abraham or not. Even those purchased as slaves were to be circumcised (17:12–13). Verse 14 adds a threat: Whoever was not circumcised would be disqualified from participating in God's promise, for "he has broken my covenant."

The commandment to circumcise all males served at least six purposes. First, it marked this group of people as distinct from other nations. This is what God meant when he referred to circumcision as a "sign" of the covenant (17:11). The act of circumcision was a ritual action that physically conveyed the covenant promises from one generation to another. As well, it would fully assimilate outsiders who joined God's people. Rituals are a means of transmitting something important. Humans often find it easier to understand spiritual matters when they are connected to something physical. Baptism involves the application of water; Communion involves partaking of bread and wine.

Second, requiring a physical act made obedience part of the covenant relationship. In order to be a part of the covenant, parents must obey God by circumcising each of their sons. It would not be enough to talk about being obedient; Abraham and his descendants would have to do something about it. Making obedience an essential part of the covenant relationship reinforced that it was, in fact, a relationship, an agreement between two parties. It also reinforced that this relationship was with One who was greater and had the right to demand obedience.

A third reason God commanded circumcision can be seen in the nature of the act as costly and painful. This graphically illustrates the sacrifice that would be involved in following him.

Fourth, God chose an act that was both familiar and unfamiliar to those in the ancient Near East. Many peoples in the ancient world practiced circumcision, albeit not in infancy or as completely as that required by God's covenant. God chose something familiar but added unique requirements to teach Abraham and his descendants that they were to be in the world but not of it. Most of what an ancient follower of Yahweh did in a typical day would have been identical to what his Canaanite neighbor did. Even many aspects of worship were similar, such as the way a person offered sacrifices and prayed. Yet there were marked differences, particularly in the understanding of God as the only God and in seeing followers as covenant partners with this God. Circumcision clearly illustrated this combination of familiar and distinctive.

Fifth, circumcision's removal of a seemingly useless piece of skin soon lent itself to a metaphorical understanding as removing an impediment, unplugging a blockage, or a clearing out (see Lev. 26:41; Jer. 9:25; Ezek. 44:7, 9). God chose a physical action that carried with it the symbolic implication that his followers should live in full fellowship with him.

Sixth, circumcision was both a public and private act. It was public in that it took place on the eighth day of a young boy's life and that it was applied to the physical organ through which the community reproduced. Yet this was obviously something very private as well, visible in adulthood only to oneself and one's wife. Likewise, the relationship of Abraham and his descendants with God was both public and private. Each person was part of the covenant community and shared in the blessings or disasters of that community. Yet each one was responsible to trust in the Lord with his or her whole heart. At his most earthy moments, each man would be reminded that he was part of the covenant community.

Circumcision continued to be an important mark of identity among Jews throughout the Old Testament period. Some relied too heavily on the act itself as evidence of covenant faithfulness and put too little emphasis on the meaning behind it, prompting Moses to command the Israelites to circumcise their hearts (Deut. 10:16), a command repeated hundreds of years later by the prophet Jeremiah (Jer. 4:4). During the Hellenistic period, when men used public baths, whether or not one was circumcised became public knowledge. Since this was a time when being Jewish might hinder one's social or political advantage or have even worse consequences, some Jews underwent surgery to reverse the procedure. The prohibition of circumcision by the Roman emperor Hadrian in the second century AD was one of the causes of the disastrous Jewish revolt.

GOD RENAMED SARAI (GEN. 17:15–22)

The narrator returned to a renaming, this time of Sarai. Once again there is no clear difference in the meaning of her new name and old name—both mean "princess." Although no word of explanation is provided, Sarai's renaming signified her new status as mother of the coming heir. Her new name, Sarah, was the same length as her old one; both have three letters in Hebrew. In Sarah, the last letter is replaced with the letter *hey*, the same letter added to Abraham's name. Both Abraham and Sarah now carried in their names a reminder of the promise that "many (*hamon*) nations" would come from their union.

After changing Sarai's name, God promised to bless her with a son, making it clear Abraham would father this son and Sarah herself would give birth to him. Verse 16 might be translated literally, "I will give from her to you a son." Although the word *blessed* (*barak*) had been used several times for Abraham, this is the first time in the Bible it is used for Sarah. God expressed his promise in beautiful poetry, translated as follows:

She will be
> for nations;
> kings of peoples
from her will be.

Abraham was delighted and surprised by this news. He fell on his face once again (17:17). For the first time in this chapter we read that Abraham spoke, though only to himself. He wondered how it would be possible for Sarah to become pregnant and bear a son at her age. The thought of it made him laugh. We do not know whether his laughter was prompted by doubt or joy. Perhaps he laughed at the inherent humor of the situation: that God would delay fulfilling his promise until now when it seemed impossible. This laugh would return later to haunt him.

Abraham's laughter quickly turned to concern. If a new child was to be heir, what would happen to Ishmael? When Abraham spoke aloud, it was in intercession (17:18). He asked whether Ishmael could "live before" God. Various translations render this differently: "live under your blessing"; "live under your special blessing" (NLT); "live in your sight" (NRSV). However translated, the meaning of Abraham's question to God seems clear enough: Why not just allow Ishmael to be the heir? Abraham may have been partly motivated by a desire to make things easier for God, but his prayer was most certainly motivated by his love for Ishmael as well.

God's answer is equally clear: No, Sarah's child will be the heir (17:19). God also provided the name they were to give to Sarah's child. By instructing them to call him Isaac, God showed that he got the joke. Isaac means "he laughs." For Abraham and Sarah, hearing their own names would be a reminder of God's promises every time they spoke Isaac's name, they would be reminded of the hilarity of their situation: an elderly, childless couple miraculously given a boy of their own.

God heard Abraham's request, however, and promised to bless Ishmael. Once again, God employed word play. His response was, "As for Ishmael, I have heard you" (17:20). Knowing that Ishmael's name means "God hears," this statement is especially meaningful.

Although he would not become the heir from whom the line would be traced, God's promise to Ishmael was generous, similar in many ways to the promises he made to Abraham and Isaac. The Hebrew word used in the phrase "make him fruitful" (17:20) is the same one used in verse 6. "Increase" and "greatly" are the same terms used in verse 2. Ishmael will become the father of a "great nation." The angel who encountered Hagar had told her that Ishmael would be the father of a nation; now we learn this nation would be great (compare 16:10). Ishmael would also become ancestor to twelve rulers. We see the fulfillment of this promise in Genesis 25:12–16. Although Ishmael's great nation and twelve rulers do not equal Abraham and Sarah's many nations and kings, God still showed great favor to Abraham's firstborn son.

The choice of Isaac over Ishmael, a later son over the firstborn, is something we see over and over in the Old Testament. God made the same choice with Jacob over Esau, Judah over Reuben, and Solomon over Adonijah. In the culture of the ancient Near East, the firstborn received more privileges than did the other children. Most important, under this system known as primogeniture, the eldest son was considered the heir. By choosing the younger over the older, God demonstrated his sovereignty over human customs. He also showed his preference for the weaker and seemingly less valuable instrument.

God wanted to make very clear that, while he loved Ishmael, his covenant would be with Isaac and his descendants. "But my covenant" (17:21) is emphatic in the original language. For the third time, God promised to "establish" this covenant (17:21). *Establish* is the same verb found in verses 7 and 19, but for the first time God provided a clear timetable of when this promised child would arrive: "by this time next year" (17:21). After twenty-four years of delay, such a promise must have seemed incredibly solid, like a firm foothold amid the swirling sands of the past decades.

Then God left (17:22). On the other occasions when he had appeared to Abraham, we understand from the context that God had left, but this is the first of only two times when the narrator specifically mentioned God's departure (see 18:33). Perhaps we are meant to understand that God has now stated all the terms of the covenant; the only thing remaining is for Abraham to obey.

CIRCUMCISION CARRIED OUT (GEN. 17:23–27)

What stands out in the remaining verses of this chapter is how promptly and comprehensively Abraham obeyed. Whatever questions may have lingered in his mind, whatever doubts or incredulity, Abraham knew what had to be done. He did it without reservation or hesitation. Every male in his household was circumcised in a single day. We do not know how many men and boys this involved, but if he had 318 fighting men at his disposal a decade or more earlier, there must have been many more than that now. All were circumcised, as well as Abraham himself and Ishmael. To do this in a single day would have been a monumental task, but such was Abraham's eagerness to uphold his end of the covenant.

Faith without works is dead, as the apostle James made clear (James 2:20). And spoken faith is inadequate and incomplete unless actions accompany it. Abraham provided a wonderful example of faith in action, quickly obeying God's command. Had Abraham not obeyed, he could not have continued as the pioneer and example of faith, nor could his life have become the paradigm of our salvation. Abraham's obedience was not in addition to his faith; it was not something he added to his belief. His obedience was an expression of his faith, the proof that his faith was alive and growing. This is why the apostle Paul used Abraham as an example of salvation by faith. From the beginning, obedience not circumcision has been the human part in the covenant. Circumcision was added as a tangible demonstration and potent symbol of one's trust in God. This is why the Old Testament presents circumcision as a symbol of obedience, encouraging people to be circumcised in their hearts as well as their bodies.

In later centuries, the spread of the gospel to non-Jews raised questions about whether Gentile believers needed to be circumcised before they could become Christians. Those who argued for circumcision likely pointed out that God called this covenant in the flesh everlasting. The early church, meeting in council in Jerusalem (Acts 15), determined this physical act was no longer necessary. A new physical act replaced it for Christians: baptism. The apostle Paul showed the connection in his letter to the Colossian Christians: "In him you were also circumcised with a circumcision not performed by human hands. Your whole self ruled by the flesh was put off when you were circumcised by Christ, having been buried with him in baptism, in which you were also raised with him through your faith in the working of God, who raised him from the dead" (Col. 2:11–12).

Abraham is the father of those who believe, serving as the pioneer of God's redemptive plan, the archetype of our salvation, and our example. Genesis 17 has provided a clear picture of Abraham in all three roles. We have seen the pioneer inaugurating the sign and seal of entry into God's covenant. In his own flesh and in the flesh of all the males of his household, Abraham was the pioneer of this ritual.

In this chapter, we saw an essential aspect of the life of all believers: Faith without works is dead. We cannot be part of God's covenant community unless we, like our archetype, prove our faith to be alive through our loving actions. How Abraham went about obeying makes him a fitting example. In spite of the challenges and pain, he promptly carried out the divine command.

CONCLUSION

Commentator Gordon Wenham speaks of Genesis 17 as a watershed. He notes that up to this point, God had been unfolding the details of his plan gradually. After this chapter, we hear fewer divine speeches and learn only a few new details, but we see more promises being fulfilled. God chose to mark this watershed moment in a significant way: by changing the names of the two principal players in the plan.[2] Also, God established the ritual act of circumcision as a way of sealing and symbolizing his covenant.

Perhaps even before the men of Abraham's camp were fully healed, God appeared to Abraham once again. He reinforced his concrete promise that Isaac would be born within the year, and used the occasion to teach Abraham and Sarah another lesson about faith. Genesis 17 may have been a watershed moment, but God had more in store for the father of our faith.

8

Responsible Grace

---◆◆◆◆---

Genesis chapters 18 and 19 each tell a very different story. The first tells of birth, the second of death. The first describes leisurely hospitality; the second, urgent escape. The first pictures God's plan unfolding in blessing; the second, God's punishment for sin. Yet each story would be incomplete without the other. The narrator skillfully weaved the accounts together to reveal not only how desperate the problem of sin is, but also how marvelous God's solution was. Together, they demonstrate divine sovereignty cooperating with human agency.

ARRIVAL OF THREE VISITORS (GEN. 18:1–8)

---◆◆◆◆---

Chapter 18 opens with Abraham sitting at the doorway of his tent at the "great trees of Mamre" (18:1) near Hebron. We learn this was the hottest part of the day. Given the hot, dry climate of Palestine, travel took place only at cooler hours. To have three visitors appear at Abraham's doorstep in the heat of the day was odd enough, but it seemed as if they had suddenly appeared out of thin air. We know from verse 1 that the arrival of these men represented a divine visitation, but Abraham was unaware, at least at first, that God himself had stopped by for lunch. Although this was not the first time God had appeared to Abraham, God had never appeared like this nor would he again.

From the first sighting of his guests, Abraham proved to be the perfect host. Although this was the hottest time of the day and he was almost one hundred years old, Abraham hurried to greet his visitors. He bowed low to the ground and invited them to stay for a meal (18:2–5). Hospitality was and remains a high priority in the Middle East. According to rabbis there, hospitality to wayfarers is greater than welcoming the Divine Presence.

Apparently, Abraham's guests gave no indication they had come to visit him specifically, for he felt it necessary to urge them to stop. "Do not pass your servant by," he implored their leader (18:3). He urged them to rest, have their feet washed, and enjoy a meal. They agreed.

Although Abraham promised only a morsel of bread, he actually served a sumptuous feast, the kind usually reserved for special occasions. There was a large quantity of fine flour, enough for each visitor to eat his fill of the best bread. There was beef of the finest and most tender quality, along with milk and something like yogurt.

In addition to emphasizing the extravagance and quality of the feast, the narrator also highlighted the haste with which these preparations were made. Abraham hurried to his guests and then to his tent, where he instructed Sarah to make the bread quickly (18:6). Then he hurried to the herd, chose the calf, and gave it to a servant. In turn the servant hurried to prepare it. In the ancient context, this was fast food. After all this hurrying, it may seem odd to see Abraham standing in the shade while his guests ate (18:8). Clearly, this meal was for them, not for him. He stood nearby so he could ensure they were carefully served and fully satisfied.

VISITORS PROMISED SARAH
WOULD HAVE A SON (GEN. 18:9–15)

At some point during or after dinner, the men inquire as to Sarah's whereabouts. This is another clue to Abraham that these were no ordinary visitors. They knew Sarah by a name she had for only a short time, perhaps just weeks or even days. Abraham answered that she was in the tent behind them. The next verse reveals she was indeed in the tent and had her ear to the tent flap, listening to what was said.

These special visitors were not just passing by; they had come specifically to convey a message to Sarah. In keeping with the etiquette of the day, they did not address her directly but delivered their message through her husband. Among the three men, one acted as spokesman and promised that Sarah would give birth to a son.

This was the second time Abraham had heard this announcement. The first had been during the events of Genesis 17. Perhaps Abraham had never told Sarah about this so the men had to bring her the message directly. Abraham may have hesitated to share the news, unsure of how she would receive it. Or perhaps he had shared it, but she found it hard to believe, so the men came to reinforce the promise. Maybe such incredible news needed to be shared more than once to allow it to sink in.

When Sarah heard she was to have a child, she laughed to herself. The narrator paused here to remind us why this news was so funny:

Abraham and Sarah were too old to have children. Sarah's silent laughter arose from the stark impossibility that she, who had already passed through menopause, could become pregnant and give birth. Would her womb, long since "worn out," be able to nurture a child through pregnancy (18:12)? The thought of all this made her laugh, but not with joy. As one commentator put it, "A life of long disappointment had taught her not to clutch at straws."[1] Hers was likely the laughter of withered hope.

Although Sarah was inside the tent and her laughter was silent, Yahweh heard. For the first time, the narrator announced what we have suspected since the guests' arrival: The spokesman is none other than Yahweh himself, and the others are angels. Yahweh had assumed a physical appearance and come to Hebron to personally announce Sarah's imminent pregnancy. Her response: to laugh incredulously. Was God enraged at her lack of faith? Would he change his mind? Would he scold her for her lack of faith?

God did not seem to be angry, and he certainly did not change his mind. If this was a divine scolding, it was a mild one. God did point out her disbelief, but he did so only to diagnose the problem. He used Sarah's laughter as an opportunity to teach Abraham (18:13–15). God showed his omniscience by telling the husband what his wife had uttered in silence. Abraham likely was reminded of his own earlier laughter (17:17). At the time, God had said nothing, so Abraham may have thought it had gone unnoticed. But if God had heard Sarah's laughter, he had certainly heard Abraham's as well, and if God was able to hear silent laughter, he could hear every thought too. Abraham understood that he was serving a God from whom there were no secrets.

God used Sarah's laughter to once again reinforce the necessity of faith. God has a great sense of humor. His ways often stretch the bounds of our credulity. He liberated his people from Egypt not by leading them away from the enemy but by backing them against the

Red Sea. Then he dried up the sea so the Israelites could pass through on dry ground and finally caused the waters to flood back and eliminate the Egyptian army. He delivered humanity from the curse of sin through a simple carpenter from Nazareth who died on a Roman cross. No wonder Paul declared that God's ways seem foolish to those who lack faith (1 Cor. 1:18), like a joke that is humorous only to those in the know. If we are to follow our spiritual father, Abraham, the archetype of our salvation, we too must believe that "the foolishness of God is wiser than human wisdom" (1 Cor. 1:25).

God instructed Abraham and Sarah to name their promised child Isaac, which means "he laughs." Why enshrine their disbelief in their son's name? Was this a punishment, a permanent painful scar to remind them never to laugh at God again? No, this was God's way of ensuring they would never forget the "foolishness" of his plan. Real faith does not deny the impossibility of an impossible situation. Real faith acknowledges how laughable it would be for God to accomplish his purpose in the face of impossible circumstances, yet trusts him anyway. God got the joke in Abraham and Sarah's situation, but wanted them to move beyond the humor of the situation to the point where they believed the impossible based on his promise alone. Otherwise, they would become stranded on the island of cynicism, unable to see anything but the chasm separating reality from God's promises.

"Is anything too hard for the LORD" (Gen. 18:14)? This may be one of the most important questions ever asked. Is God really more powerful than any obstacle? Jeremiah faced this question in his prophetic ministry. God instructed him to purchase land outside Jerusalem just as the Babylonians were poised to conquer the city. Jeremiah obeyed the Lord, but it must have seemed ridiculous to spend money on land that would soon be worthless. When he appealed for an explanation, God responded, "I am the LORD, the

God of all mankind. Is anything too hard for me?" (Jer. 32:27). God would allow the Babylonians to conquer Judah but would later accomplish his purpose so that "once more fields will be bought in this land" (Jer. 32:43).

"Is anything too hard for the Lord?" is a rhetorical question; the assumed answer is an emphatic, "No!" However, any who would follow in faith must answer this question not in a classroom but in real life. Each of us must determine if we will continue to trust God when his promise sounds like a joke.

God summoned Abraham and Sarah to move to this level of trust by reasserting that the promised child would be born around this time in the following year (compare Gen. 17:21). God repeated his previous promise and, as he had done so often before, revealed a new detail: "I will return to you at the appointed time next year" (18:14). God announced that this birth would be a miracle from conception to delivery. Even though he was revealing the details of his plan with the highest degree of specificity to date, God was also forcing Abraham and Sarah to choose whether to laugh it off as impossible or believe that a year from now they would be cradling their newborn son.

ANNOUNCEMENT ABOUT SODOM (GEN. 18:16–21)

The transition from Sarah's laughter to the following scene seems abrupt. What connection can there be between the thrilling announcement of Isaac's birth and the terrible destiny of the Sodomites? These stories, cast side by side, provide a contrast between light and darkness, life and death, hope and condemnation, blessing and destruction. If we consider only God's treatment of Sodom, we might cower in the presence of such a righteous deity. However, having learned of the promise of Isaac and knowing what this implies about God's unfolding plan of redemption, we recognize that the story of Sodom's destruction would not be God's last word. He had a plan that would mean the end of the problem of sin, a plan already in process through Abraham and his soon-to-be born son, Isaac.

The connection between these two stories becomes clearer as we overhear the private conversation among Abraham's visitors (18:16–19). Lunch had concluded, and the travelers were starting on their way while Abraham was walking alongside. Yahweh turned to the other two and asked whether they should bring Abraham into their confidence. Yahweh was not asking for advice; his question was designed to introduce his reasons for involving Abraham in his plans. First, Abraham would "surely become a great and powerful nation" (18:18). By saying this, God added new information to the earlier announcements about Abraham's descendants being numerous; they would also be powerful. The founder of such a great and powerful nation should have the opportunity to understand God's feelings about sin.

Second, Abraham and his offspring were to be a channel of blessing for all nations (18:18). Against the looming destruction of the Sodomites, such a promise of blessing shone brightly. It was precisely for this reason—to be a source of blessing—that God chose Abraham as the pioneer of God's redemptive plan. And this was the third reason for bringing the patriarch into his confidence. The verb *chosen* literally means "to know." God announced that he had made Abraham his friend. In the words of one commentator, God "singled him out."[2] God would use this same verb in verse 21 to describe his investigation of Sodom. The repetition of this verb conveys a picture of a God with a plan, moving purposefully to bring it about.

God's fourth reason for telling Abraham about the fate of Sodom was that it would better enable the patriarch to accomplish the purpose for which he had been chosen by teaching his sons and household to obey God by doing what is right and just (18:19). Abraham was a quick learner, for he soon employed the second term, *just*, in his negotiations with God (18:25 ESV).

All that follows in Genesis 18–19 is part of God's curriculum to prepare Abraham for his role. He heard God speak of investigating the outcry against Sodom and Gomorrah and watched as the two angels left on their reconnaissance mission. A God who could hear unspoken thoughts behind tent flaps must already have known what was going on in Sodom. This "investigation" was more about showing Abraham that God acts only when all the facts are in, never on hearsay.

Only after the wickedness of the cities had been clearly established (see 19:4–14) would God bring about the judgment sin deserved. The next morning, when Abraham saw smoke rise from the plain (19:28), he understood more clearly the importance of maintaining a righteous family line. He saw firsthand the seriousness of sin and God's determination to punish it. Whether or not Abraham understood the full scope of God's redemptive plan, he did recognize that becoming a blessing to the nations in some sense meant providing an antidote to the disease that had befallen the Sodomites.

Here we see another connection with the preceding story. The earlier account concerned the birth of Isaac, a crucial link in the divine plan. Immediately after making his most specific promise regarding Isaac's birth, God reminded Abraham that this child was part of an important plan. God made it clear that his plan was not just about Abraham, Sarah, and Isaac, but also about solving the problem of sin. Isaac's birth was a cause for laughter, yet his purpose in life was not merely to provide pleasure for his parents, but to further God's redemptive plan. When Lot warned his sons-in-law of the coming destruction, they "thought he was joking" (19:14). *Joking* is a form of the same word used for Isaac's name. The repetition of the term reminds us that while God's plan brings great joy, the story of sin is no laughing matter.

God did not intend for Abraham to be a silent spectator to this lesson on divine justice. After the angels left, God paused to give time for Abraham to speak. Many scholars agree that the narrator originally wrote, "But Yahweh remained standing before Abraham." Later copyists perhaps thought describing God as waiting for Abraham was irreverent, so they changed the text to the form that appears in many translations: "Abraham remained standing before the LORD" (18:22). More likely, God waited, knowing Abraham wanted to negotiate on Sodom's behalf and wanting him to do just that.

We do not know for certain what prompted Abraham to intercede on behalf of the Sodomites, but it may have been concern for his nephew. Notably, however, Abraham did not appeal on behalf of Lot alone, but for the entire city. This is the third time the narrator specifically described Abraham speaking with God (see 15:2, 8). In the first two instances, Abraham made appeals for himself or his family. This time it was for strangers.

By allowing Abraham to negotiate for the deliverance of strangers, God affirmed his love for all humanity. Inclusion into God's covenant community sometimes brings the temptation to be exclusive. This can be seen in the book of Jonah and throughout the history of Christianity. We may be tempted to only care about others if they are "one of us." In doing so, we fail to recognize that, first and foremost, people are human beings created in God's image. Abraham knew the Sodomites were sinful, but he took the risk of appealing to God on their behalf. We need never choose between faithfulness and kindness.

Earlier, God asked the important rhetorical question: "Is any-thing too hard for the LORD?" (18:14). During these negotiations, Abraham also asked a rhetorical question: "Will not the Judge of all the earth do right?" (18:25). By combining these two questions, we have the complete truth of God's character. The first question is essential because it asserts God's limitless power. But how will he use that power? What if he wields it arbitrarily, disregarding right? Without a clear assurance of God's justice, his power is only fright-ening. The second rhetorical question provides the necessary qual-ification. God's power is limitless, but he will employ it only in doing what is right, good, just, and fair.

Do not miss the point that we see this clearer picture of God only because of divine-human synergy. Both God and Abraham con-tributed to this conversation and thereby to our understanding. Abra-ham, as one commentator wrote, "was no yes-man, but a true partner."[3] All that Abraham did and said was based on grace. Had God not taken the initiative, Abraham could not have contributed anything. He would not even be talking to God if God had not first graciously summoned him from Harran. Yet because of God's grace, Abraham became a full participant in the divine plan. Faith requires boldness, not only to face the impossibilities of our situation, but also to enter into God's work and accomplish what he sovereignly and graciously assigned. Grace makes us responsible.

Of course, we must responsibly exercise this responsibility. Abra-ham provided a great example of that as he felt his way forward by faith. We have already noted how his selfless love expressed itself in concern for total strangers — and sinful ones at that. As well, Abraham was genuinely humble. He readily acknowledged that his participation with God was possible only by grace (see 18:27, 30–32). Yet he was also bold. He appealed to God to spare Sodom six times. Twice in verse 25 he employed the expression, "Far be it from you," even though he addressed God himself. He took God at his word that the "way of the LORD" involves "doing what is right and just" (18:19). He held God accountable to live up to his own standard. Faith works best when love, humility, and boldness nourish it well.

INVESTIGATION AND JUDGMENT ON
SODOM AND GOMORRAH (GEN. 19:1–29)

Although Abraham does not appear until the very end of this section, the scene reveals his character as contrasted with that of his nephew. When Lot first settled at Sodom, it was in a tent on the outskirts of the city (13:12). Then he moved to a house within the city walls. By the time the angels arrived, he had become a leader in the city. The angels encountered him in the gate (19:1), where city elders usually sat. Lot was fully aware of the sinfulness of his city. He insisted the visitors spend the night at his house because he knew how they would be treated otherwise. Lot's decision to dwell in this city and his reluctance to leave it (19:16) sharply contrast with his uncle who maintained a healthy distance from the sinfulness of his Canaanite neighbors, Sodom in particular (14:22–23). We also note the difference in hospitality shown by Abraham and Lot. Lot was generous to his visitors (19:3), but not as generous as his uncle had been (compare 18:6–8). Lot's hospitality took an ugly turn when he had to choose between the safety of his guests and that of his daughters (19:6–8).

Lot's characteristic emotion throughout this story was fear—fear that he would not survive his journey to the mountains (19:18–20), then fear of what would happen should he remain in Zoar (19:30). The incest that concludes Genesis 19 arose directly as a consequence of Lot's fear. By contrast, Abraham is a picture of courage, whether battling the northern coalition, refusing an alliance with the king of Sodom, or encountering Yahweh. His courage allowed God to provide Abraham with progeny that would bless all nations.

We see another contrast between Abraham and Lot in the intercession offered by the two. The uncle appealed for the whole city to be spared for the sake of others. Lot appealed for those in the tiny hamlet of Zoar, but only for his own sake (19:20). Lot's appeal, though granted, was unnecessary, since God had already promised to protect him until he reached the mountains (19:21). Abraham's appeal, while unsuccessful on a larger scale, was granted in that God "remembered Abraham" by sparing Lot's life (19:29). Abraham had not specifically appealed for Lot's life, only for the city to be spared if there were ten righteous men. There were not even that many, but God's grace always gives us more than we ask for.

The narrator returned to Abraham in verse 27 and focused on him and his descendants throughout the rest of Genesis. The last we read of Lot in the book of Genesis is the sordid tale included in 19:30–38. In Genesis 13, we noted how Lot had chosen the best land, leaving his uncle with second best. Here we see what happens when one chooses short-term happiness over long-term trust. The best land became desolate as Lot escaped with just the robe on his back. His family developed in a dysfunctional fashion, and his offspring kept moving farther from the Promised Land. Eventually, Lot's descendants became some of Israel's most determined enemies. By contrast, Abraham continued to wait for the promised blessings. In hindsight we can see how much wiser he was to choose long-term trust over immediate gain.

CONCLUSION

The stories in Genesis 18–19 belong together. They combine to present a clear picture of sin's devastating effect along with the promise of its eventual destruction through God's redemptive plan. In these stories, we discover that while God can do anything he chooses, he will employ his power only in ways that are just and right. We are left with a picture of the divine-human synergy that reflects responsible grace.

By now we have come to expect Abraham to stumble immediately after a triumph of faith, so we should not be surprised by what happens next. What is surprising is how grace continued to be offered during one of Abraham's weakest moments.

9

Surprising Grace

—◆—✦—◆—

GENESIS 20

We are happy to leave behind the smell of smoke and brimstone that surrounded what had been Sodom and travel with Abraham to Gerar. Challenges awaited the patriarch in this new setting, and they were challenges of his own making. Here he would learn even more about God's plan, particularly how this plan operates by grace, not by merit. Because God is motivated solely by grace, he can display himself to whomever he chooses, whether they are his covenant people or not. Abraham would also discover that God works through weak human instruments. He would be challenged to embrace this surprising grace and come to see God at work anywhere and everywhere, even within the heart of the patriarch himself.

ABIMELEK TOOK SARAH (GEN. 20:1–7)

As a nomad, Abraham was obliged to move his flocks, herds, and household to wherever there was sufficient pasturage. This may explain why he left the area of Hebron to travel south into the Negev region. There he spent time between the oasis of Kadesh and the Egyptian town of Shur before entering the territory of Gerar. Unlike his earlier trip to Egypt, this excursion did not take Abraham beyond the land God had promised, which extended "from the Wadi of Egypt to the great river, the Euphrates" (15:18). (The Wadi of Egypt refers not to the Nile River, but to a smaller brook just south of the Promised Land.) Although the land would someday belong to Abraham's descendants, at the time it belonged to other nations. The Philistines, under Abimelek, ruled the territory where Abraham camped.

The Philistines, who later caused such trouble for Saul and David (as well as other nations in the ancient Near East, such as Egypt and the Hittites), arrived in Canaan several centuries after Abraham, around 1200 BC. The narrator might have applied this name anachronistically to an unrelated group that preceded the Philistines but occupied the same region, or Abimelek and his people may have come to the land in an earlier, less overwhelming wave of Philistine migration. In either case, Abraham's status among them was that of a sojourner or resident alien, who lacked legal rights and was vulnerable to oppression by the land's inhabitants.

Once again, Abraham feared for his safety and lied about Sarah (20:2). He had made this mistake before and experienced the near-disastrous consequences. Had he not learned his lesson? It may help to remember that the Egyptian fiasco had occurred a quarter of a century earlier. The ruse had left him richer, while the sting of humiliation may have long since dissipated. God gave humans the ability to forget or remember selectively, but this gift has a dark side as well. If any recollection of his shame remained in Abraham's mind, it was eclipsed by his terror at what the inhabitants of Gerar might do to him. We must continually exercise faith or it will weaken. As one commentator notes, "One of the first evidences of weakening faith is a loss of discernment."[1] This is not the first time a stumble followed a high water mark of Abraham's faith. His failure in Egypt followed his faith-filled departure from Harran (12:1–9). His misjudgment regarding Hagar followed his incredible vision of the torch and smoking firepot (chs. 15–16). We are often most vulnerable to the Enemy just after a great victory.

This passage also raises a surprising question: What could the king of Gerar find attractive about a ninety-year-old woman? As we suggested in our discussion of the incident in Egypt, beauty is a culturally determined value so we cannot assume the same standards of beauty applied then as they do now. Some have suggested that Sarah had retained her beauty as the result of the physical changes associated with her present or imminent pregnancy. The text, however, does not mention her beauty. It may be that Sarah's most attractive feature was the fact that her "brother" was a wealthy and powerful nomad. Abimelek made an economic and political decision, not necessarily a romantic one, and added Sarah to his harem (20:2).

Now what would become of God's plan? If Sarah was not already pregnant with Isaac, there would be no way for Abraham to father the child with her, as multiple divine promises had predicted. If she was pregnant, the child would become Abimelek's, not Abraham's, and this fact would negate still more promises. Even if these events could somehow be immediately undone, a shadow of doubt about his true parentage would likely hang over Isaac's head. Thanks to Abraham's cowardice, God's plan had reached a dead end.

However, the events that followed reveal God as sovereign not only over Abraham, but even over a Gentile king. Shortly after Sarah entered Abimelek's harem, something went terribly wrong in Gerar. None of the women in the king's household, either his wives or his slave girls, could conceive. We don't know for sure if the problem was female infertility or male impotence. However, the latter is more likely because when Abraham interceded, it was Abimelek (not the women) who was healed (20:17).

Around this time God appeared to the king in a dream. We might better call it a nightmare because it began by God announcing to Abimelek, "You are as good as dead" (20:3). The king had committed a capital offense against another man by taking his wife. Making matters worse, the offended man was a mighty prophet. If Abimelek did not immediately return Sarah to Abraham, the king would die.

Abimelek defended himself by asserting that Abraham and Sarah had deceived him. Both of them had lied to him. The king also appealed to God's sense of justice. It would not be fair, he claimed, to destroy an innocent nation for this accidental offense (20:4). Abimelek's reference to the nation seems out of place because, up to this point, God had threatened only the life of the king. Some suggest *nation* should be rendered more generally as *people*, so that verse 4 would read something like, "Do you go around killing innocent people?" More likely Abimelek was concerned about the nation he ruled as king. This is supported by the reference to the plural *you* in verse 7 and to "my kingdom" in verse 9. In the ancient Near East, the king was often compared to a shepherd and his people to a flock. To "strike the shepherd" meant the "sheep will be scattered" (Zech. 13:7).

The narrator informed us that Abimelek had not "gone near" Sarah (Gen. 20:4), which was likely a euphemism suggesting that they had not had sexual intercourse. The same phrase is used this way several times in the Old Testament (compare Lev. 18:6; Deut. 22:14). The king had probably tried to have sex with Sarah but was unable to do so. God informed Abimelek that this was his doing: "I have kept you from sinning against me. That is why I did not let you touch her" (Gen. 20:6).

Abimelek asserted his blamelessness, saying, "With purity of heart and innocence of hands I have done this" (20:5, literal translation), an assertion God promptly affirmed. Some commentators fault Abimelek for not acknowledging that he had forcibly abducted Sarah, but there is no evidence that Sarah had been abducted, forcibly or otherwise. While she did not join the king's harem of her own volition, it was Abraham who was to blame, not Abimelek. God showed his justice by giving the king a way to escape impending doom. He also showed his omniscience in that he knew the king's heart (20:6). As well, God showed his grace by preventing Abimelek from making matters worse.

Taking another man's wife was bad enough, but taking one from a powerful prophet was downright dangerous (20:7). When we hear the term *prophet*, we think of someone who predicts the future and look in vain for any such predictions by Abraham. However, in the ancient Near East, this term did not necessarily imply making predictions. A prophet was a man or woman who served as a conduit for divine power, whether by predicting the future or in some other way. A prophet was so powerful that to sin against him was equivalent to sinning against God. Remember what God said to Abimelek: "I have kept you from sinning against me" (20:6). How fitting that the first person in the Bible to be called a prophet is Abraham, the pioneer, archetype, and example of our faith. How ironic that this term applied to him while he was cowering in fear instead of depending on God's power.

Alerting the king to Abraham's true identity accomplished at least two purposes. First, it discouraged Abimelek from even thinking of retaliating against Abraham. Instead, the king realized he must handle this situation very carefully so as not to further offend this powerful man. Second, it gave Abimelek some hope that his impotence problem would be solved. The prayer of a powerful prophet would likely do the trick.

ABIMELEK CONFRONTED ABRAHAM AND MADE AMENDS (GEN. 20:8–16)

The king got up early the next morning to make amends. Throughout the Old Testament, waking early indicates sincerity and earnestness for the task at hand. We last read this idiom when Abraham rose early to see what had happened to Sodom overnight (19:27). Rather than immediately summoning Abraham, however, the king first called in his counselors (20:8). Apparently he wanted to make sure everyone was aware of Abraham's special status so no one would further offend him. After that, he called for Abraham.

Abraham's carefully crafted but lame attempt at self-justification suggests that he knew why he was being summoned so early in the morning to Abimelek's throne room. The king blasted Abraham with three questions and one very strong assertion (20:9–10). The first two questions were rhetorical, alerting Abraham to the serious dangers his lie had set in motion. The king first asked Abraham to consider the dangerous predicament he had brought on Abimelek and his people. Next, the king asked what he had done to provoke Abraham. Abimelek used the same verb here (*wronged*) that God used in verse 6 to describe what the king had nearly done (*sinning*) against God. These questions reveal that Abraham had thought only of himself, not of Abimelek or the nation of Gerar. How different he seems from the man who repeatedly interceded for the people of Sodom, and how remote from the man who was to be a source of blessing to all nations.

Abimelek next accused Abraham of doing something against him "that should never be done" (20:9). This wording indicates that Abraham had violated the basic laws of civility. The New Living Translation captures it well: "No one should ever do what you have done!" How different Abraham was now from the consummate host in Genesis 18.

The king asked a third question, this time one he expected Abraham to answer. "What was your reason for doing this?" might literally be translated as "What did you see?" (20:10). A prophet was supposed to be divinely endowed to see what others could not. This is why a prophet was sometimes called a seer. Abimelek assumed this prophet must have seen something in the king or his people that prompted such harsh treatment.

Abraham's answer is embarrassing. He said he saw "no fear of God in this place" (20:11). The response of Abimelek and his officials clearly demonstrated their fear of God. When confronted, Abimelek immediately repented, defended his actions as unintentional, and made amends—proof that he feared God. His officials were "very much afraid" when they learned what had happened (20:8). Abraham said he saw no fear of God in these people, but it was Abraham who feared the people so much that he failed to trust God. Abraham had less fear of God than they did. This seer was not good at seeing. The narrator strengthened this point with a play on words: the Hebrew verbs *to see* and *to fear* are almost identical.

Rather than turning to God for protection, Abraham took matters into his own hands. This powerful prophet, who had already interceded for a sinful city (Gen. 18), put innocent people in harm's way when he felt personally threatened. In the last chapter, we applauded

Abraham's ability to show concern for those beyond his own family. His example here suggests he had not yet fully embraced his role as the one by whom God would bless all nations. When push came to shove, Abraham's first priority remained Abraham.

To his embarrassing self-defense, Abraham added a limp half-truth. Yes, Sarah was his half-sister (20:12), but this completely sidestepped the more important fact that she was his wife, whom he had treated recklessly and shamefully. And he had the nerve to blame God. It was he who had called Abraham to become a wanderer, subjecting him to these dangerous situations. As a way of protecting himself, Abraham made it his policy to resort to deception (20:13). This explanation told Abimelek that this near catastrophe was nothing personal. It also revealed how much fear remained in the father of those who believe.

According to verse 14, Abimelek brought livestock and servants and gave them to Abraham. With these gifts, Abimelek provided a formal, public settlement and insured that Abraham, the mighty prophet, would do nothing to harm him. The previous time Abraham passed off his wife as his sister, he also received a tremendous gift: a dowry. That gift was for damages. In both cases, God had graciously turned Abraham's failure to a blessing.

Next the king offered Abraham the opportunity to settle anywhere in his land. Pharaoh had done the opposite, evicting Abraham from Egypt as nothing more than a pesky foreigner. Abimelek reasoned that having Abraham around would be a good thing. He was, after all, a powerful prophet who could help ensure Gerar's safety and strength. Intuitively, the king acknowledged what God had promised: Those whom Abraham blesses would be blessed (12:3). Abimelek would later make this acknowledgment explicit (see 21:22).

Then the king turned to Sarah and publicly vindicated her by giving Abraham one thousand shekels of silver (20:16). Most translations render the term *vindicated* or something synonymous because the Hebrew word can have this meaning and it better fits the context. Sarah might have shared some of Abraham's guilt and therefore needed to be reproved, but Abimelek's gift to her husband of a thousand shekels does not seem like much of a scolding.

The phrase "cover the offense" (20:16) is an idiom that literally means "cover the eyes." It implies that no one will have reason to look into the matter further. The king referred to Abraham as Sarah's "brother" (20:16) rather than her husband perhaps to avoid publicly embarrassing her, or suggesting a tinge of frustration on the king's part. Abimelek's public defense of Sarah's innocence along with the earlier acknowledgements that the couple did not have sexual intercourse eliminated any doubt that Abraham was the father of the child she would soon bear.

GOD HEALED ABIMELEK'S HOUSEHOLD IN RESPONSE TO ABRAHAM'S PRAYER (GEN. 20:17–18)

In the closing scene of this story, we find Abraham interceding on behalf of Abimelek and his household. This is not the only instance in the Old Testament where someone who has been offended intercedes for those who have offended him. After Miriam and Aaron challenged Moses' leadership and Miriam was struck with leprosy, Moses quickly called on God to heal Miriam, and God responded (Num. 12:1–15). God instructed Job to pray for his three friends who so badly misjudged him. When Job prayed, God responded (Job 42:7–9). We have no record of Abraham praying for Pharaoh. This may have been God's intention, but the proud Egyptian king had chosen to expel his intercessor (Gen. 12:17–20). We do have another instance of Abraham interceding; his negotiations on behalf of Sodom (18:16–33) are a model of intercessory prayer. How different the circumstances were this time. Before, Abraham took it upon himself to "sit across the table" from the Lord and appeal for a whole city. Now, his intercession was mandatory and amounted to cleaning up his own mess.

As usual, God was teaching Abraham and his spiritual offspring several important lessons. By requiring him to be part of the solution to the problems he had created, Abraham would have felt a measure of guilt and shame. This was a mild form of punishment, but it was probably sufficient in a heart as genuine as Abraham's. Having to clean up the mess that results from depending on oneself instead of God reinforces how important it is to "trust in the LORD with all your heart and lean not on your own understanding; in all your ways submit to him and he will make your paths straight" (Prov. 3:5–6). Perhaps Abraham learned his lesson. We are not privy to all the events of his life from this point on, but we never again read that he employed the "she is my sister" ruse.

God may have used Abraham as part of the solution to reinforce another important truth: God is the God of all people, not just Abraham's family. When the patriarch entered Gerar, he seemed cynical about whether others could fear God. Perhaps his cynicism arose from his failed intercession on behalf of Sodom. "If there were not even ten righteous people in that city," he may have reasoned, "there may not be any here either." He said, "There is surely no fear of God in this place" (Gen. 20:11), when the opposite was actually true. Abimelek and his officials were quick to fear and obey God. By reenlisting Abraham to intercede for another nation, God was demonstrating that he cared about all people, and would go to great lengths to help them.

Abraham's intercession was a source of blessing to Abimelek and the nation of Gerar, just as God had promised. Granted, the way in which God chose to bless others through Abraham is a bit surprising. We tend to lock God into certain ways of working, but he delights in bursting out of our boxes. The incarnation of Christ may be the best example of God's tendency to surprise us. In unexpected ways and employing flawed agents, God demonstrates his sovereign grace.

God had another lesson for Abraham, one that may have been painful to learn. Although Abraham's prayers could open the wombs of other women, they could not do so for his own wife. Why was this? God did not explain. His ways are higher than ours; his plans are not our plans. Abraham needed to recognize this truth if he were to be the pioneer of God's redemptive plan. Fortunately, Abraham did learn this lesson. Later, when God commanded the unimaginable, Abraham obeyed, believing God had his own reasons (see Gen. 22; Heb. 11:19).

This is an important lesson for us as well. Because of our cultural context, we assume that we can solve all our problems. Certainly God has blessed us with amazing scientific and technological knowledge so we can solve many of the problems that have afflicted humanity for millennia. Problems such as disease, ignorance, and food shortages are still with us, though, in spite of our progress. Our scientific and technological knowledge has created the temptation to put too much emphasis on human knowledge and ability. We may be more susceptible than previous generations to forget who God is and who he is not. Such idolatry has its extreme forms, such as rank materialism, licentious hedonism, or angry atheism. More dangerous to believers are the subtler forms this forgetfulness takes. We often demand from God an explanation for the suffering we are forced to endure. We doubt God's ability to be more powerful in a situation than we are. We treat God's Word as if we could plumb its depths by employing human reasoning. We must face similar challenges Abraham faced if we are to be his spiritual children: "Who has known the mind of the Lord? Or who has been his counselor?" (Rom. 11:34).

Requiring Abraham to intercede on behalf of those he had harmed reinforced yet another lesson: the consequences of sin. Sin was the problem for which God's plan was the solution. Even though Abraham did not fully understand this plan, it would eventually eliminate the need for fear and doubt that had landed him in this situation. God also wanted to teach a lesson on grace to Abraham and those for whom he serves as archetype. If the patriarch could still successfully intercede for others even after he had caused their problem, the power of the intercessor's prayers must proceed from someone other than himself. We must understand that our best efforts and the motivation to employ prayers do not originate within ourselves. They too are a gift from God. Therefore, we cannot earn God's favor by our deeds. God graciously chose to use Abraham not because he was a perfect man, but because he was willing to be faithful. Give God a willing heart, and he will do the rest.

CONCLUSION

Apparently, Abraham accepted the king's gracious offer to dwell in Gerar. More importantly, the patriarch settled in with a new understanding of God's grace which he had made known to foreign kings and frail humans. Abraham would need this new understanding, for shortly he would encounter both the fulfillment of God's promise of a son and the difficult repercussions this birth would set in motion.

10

God Is Eternal

GENESIS 21

Finally, the long awaited moment had arrived. The promised child was born, and Abraham's household filled with laughter at the birth of the little boy named "he laughs." It was not long, however, before laughter turned to jealousy, then to conflict, and ultimately to heartache and alienation. God's plan had given birth not only to Abraham's pleasure, but also his pain. Soon after the birth of his son, the patriarch was forced to deal with his grief over Ishmael, and at that very moment he faced conflict from another front, Abimelek. This, too, was the result of divine favor. God had kept his promise to bless Abraham, but those blessings left him exposed. He needed land and wells to feed and water his four-footed "blessings," but the land and water belonged to powerful people. Abraham had to deal with the conflict that surrounded him if he was to be the pioneer of God's redemptive plan. Throughout Genesis 21, the patriarch once again serves as the archetype for our own relationship with God and models the kind of faith that can navigate turbulent waters.

BIRTH OF ISAAC (GEN. 21:1-7)

The narrator left no doubt that Isaac's arrival was nothing short of miraculous. It was clearly God's doing. "Was gracious to" (21:1) represents a Hebrew word that implies divine intervention in human affairs for an important reason. The narrator further highlighted the significance of Isaac's birth by mentioning Yahweh's name twice in the first verse, the first time in an emphatic position. Three times in the opening two verses the narrator reminded us that this birth took place in fulfillment of God's promise: "as he had said"; "what he had promised"; and "at the very time God had promised him" (21:1-2). The third phrase adds that the birth occurred precisely when God said it would (see 17:21; 18:10, 14).

Another clue that this birth was extraordinary is the repeated mention that the child was born to parents too old to produce a child: "to Abraham in his old age" (21:2); "to the son Sarah bore him" (21:3); "Abraham was a hundred years old when his son Isaac was born to him" (21:5); "in his old age" (21:7). The Hebrew verb meaning "to bear" appears four times in these verses. One translation renders verse 3 more literally: "Abraham called the name of his son who was born to him, whom Sarah bore to him, Isaac" (NASB). One commentator describes these verses as expressing "the quiet precision of [God's] control."[1]

In addition to God's sovereignty, the narrator emphasized the patriarch's complete obedience. Abraham named the boy Isaac, as God had commanded. Unlike that of the other patriarchs, Isaac's name would remain unchanged throughout his lifetime. Abraham also dutifully circumcised his son on the eighth day, according to God's command.

These verses also provide a lovely picture of Sarah's reaction to Isaac's birth. We catch her sense of humor as she makes a pun on Isaac's name. "God has brought me laughter" (21:6) literally means "laughter God has made for me." God had formed little "he laughs" in her once-barren womb, then made her laugh after her little boy was born. Her laughter that had once been ironic and incredulous was now unabridged and open. Laughter once expressed only privately in the recesses of the heart was now available for all to share: "Everyone who hears about this will laugh with me" (21:6). Sarah spoke more truly than she knew, for her child was to become the key player in the crucial next step of the plan that would eventually bring joy to the world through Christ.

HAGAR AND ISHMAEL WERE SENT AWAY (GEN. 21:8–21)

Isaac was born because God had kept his promise, but Isaac's birth forced the issue of Abraham's succession. The question came to a head at a great party thrown to celebrate Isaac's weaning (21:8). (Children in this culture would nurse until they were two or three years old.) By this time, Ishmael would have been at least fifteen years old. In the midst of this joyous celebration, Sarah saw something that turned her laughter into ferocious jealousy.

Exactly what Sarah saw is unclear. Perhaps in Sarah's eyes Ishmael was not showing proper respect to the rightful heir. He may have been mocking the fuss being made over Isaac or taunting his little brother with the fact that he, Ishmael, was the firstborn son. He may have been trying to get some attention on a day when all eyes were on his little brother. Perhaps he was only doing what he heard the grown-ups do many times before: joke about Isaac's name. The mocking may have been more serious, perhaps being harmful. The apostle Paul referred to Ishmael as having "persecuted" Isaac (Gal. 4:29).

Another possibility is that the Hebrew verb rendered "mocking" should be translated more innocently as "playing." This is how two very early versions translate the word. The two are the Septuagint, a rendering of the Hebrew Bible into Greek that was completed in the second and third centuries before Christ, and the Vulgate, an important translation of the Bible into Latin prepared in the fourth century after Christ. This is also how this verb is understood by an early retelling of Genesis prepared in the years between the events of the Old and New Testaments. Jubilees 17:4 explains that what made Sarah so jealous was seeing "Ishmael playing and dancing, and Abraham rejoicing with great joy."[2]

If the verb is rendered as mocking or persecuting, Sarah's reaction made sense. If Ishmael was only guilty of playing with his brother, however, why did Sarah react so strongly? Perhaps the sight of Abraham rejoicing made her jealous. She refused to share Abraham with anyone's son but her own. Or it may be that, as she watched the boys at play, Sarah realized that Abraham would have to face the question of who would inherit the promises. As hard as it would be for Abraham to part with Ishmael, she knew the relationship between the two boys would only get worse with time.

The question of whether the verb means mocking or playing is impossible to answer. Whatever its immediate cause, Sarah's concern symbolized a looming conflict whose profundity extended well beyond boisterous brotherly play. Abraham was the archetype of God's plan of salvation, which means the essence of his experience reflects the experience of every believer. The apostle Paul made it clear that these two brothers represented two ways of encountering God. Ishmael symbolized the "flesh" (Gal. 4:23, 29), the path of human design and human construction. Ishmael was born from the scheme hatched by Sarah and affirmed by Abraham. This scheme was the best they could manage in their attempt to further God's plan.

Isaac, on the other hand, was born as the result of a "promise" (Gal. 4:23, 28), "by the power of the Spirit" (Gal. 4:29). Paul made the point that God's redemptive plan proceeds only by divine promise and power. Human effort, though it can accomplish some good, cannot overcome the vast breach created by sin. Only God's grace working through the Holy Spirit can reconcile us to God, one another, ourselves, and the natural world. Isaac's birth precipitated this conflict between flesh and promise, but Isaac's birth was also part of God's plan to bring about the reconciliation of all humankind.

It is unlikely that all this flashed before Sarah's eyes that day, but she saw enough to convince her that Hagar and her son must leave the household immediately. She demanded that Abraham "get rid" (Gen. 21:10) of them—disinherit Hagar and Ishmael by granting them their freedom. Perhaps Sarah even quoted God's earlier promise to her husband: "A son who is your own flesh and blood will be your heir" (15:4). Her motives, however, appear to be less about honoring God and more about protecting Isaac. Note how she referred to Ishmael, not by name or even as Abraham's son, but as "her son," that is, the son of "that slave woman" Hagar (21:10). A more literal translation of the end of verse 10 highlights her loyalties: "The son of this slave woman will never share in the inheritance with my son, with Isaac."

Sarah's demand deeply "distressed" Abraham (21:11). He knew that by sending Ishmael away, he was putting the entirety of his future in Isaac's hands. What if something should happen to Isaac? What would he do for an heir? How would the promise continue? He was also distressed because he dearly loved Ishmael and dreaded the thought of losing him. Witnessing his agony, one can only imagine how difficult it was for him to obey God's command in the next chapter regarding Isaac. Very likely God used the experience of letting go of Ishmael to prepare Abraham for the later, greater challenge. With God, no sorrow or challenge is useless, but fits into a larger, greater plan.

Although Abraham hated to comply with Sarah's demand, he may have felt a sense of obligation to do so, given what he had put her through with Abimelek. More compelling was his own sense that sending Ishmael away was the right thing. By now God had made it very clear that Isaac would be Abraham's heir (18:10, 14). The longer Ishmael remained, the more difficult things would become between the brothers. Abraham also had confidence that God had great plans for Ishmael as well (17:20).

As Abraham wrestled with his decision, God appeared to him. God had not appeared with instructions the last time Abraham considered a proposal from Sarah. Perhaps Yahweh knew how difficult this decision was for Abraham and made it easier by directly communicating his will. God also knew that whatever Sarah's motives were in demanding the expulsion of Hagar and her son, she was right. Abraham needed to send Ishmael away. God assured Abraham that no harm would come to Isaac because the line would continue through him (21:12). Nor should he worry about Ishmael. Thus, God reaffirmed his earlier promises and assured Abraham that he would also make his firstborn, Ishmael, into a great nation (21:12–13).

Abraham woke early the next morning to set about his heart-rending task. The phrase "early the next morning" (21:14) likely suggests his hope to send Hagar and Ishmael off before the heat of the day. It also affirms Abraham's "habit of facing a hard task resolutely."[3] He would also arise early on the morning he would take Isaac to Mount Moriah.

Abraham's actions demonstrated compassion for mother and child. He provided them with food and water, even putting the supplies on Hagar's shoulders himself. Although the water ran out, Abraham was not to blame. Water is heavy to carry—each gallon weighs about eight pounds, not including the weight of the container—so Abraham probably loaded her with as much as she could carry.

And it was enough water to get them to the next well (21:19). We also see Abraham's compassion in that he "sent her off" (21:14), a phrase used to describe emancipation and something milder than Sarah's "get rid of" (21:10).

The last time Hagar left Abraham's camp, she appeared to head south toward Egypt. This time she headed southeast toward Beersheba. She may have been trying to reach a spur route that would take her south to the Way of Shur, a major road leading to Egypt. Another possible destination was Arabia. Hagar had earlier learned from God that her son would be a nomad (16:12), so she may have been traveling to a place suitable for that lifestyle.

When she reached the desert of Beersheba, Hagar became lost. She wandered until her water ran out, then she gave up in despair. Thinking she and Ishmael were both going to die in the wilderness, she put Ishmael under a bush (21:15). The Hebrew verb rendered *put* is elsewhere translated *throw* or *cast*. It seems unlikely that Hagar could throw a fifteen-year-old boy very far. The verb has a range of meanings that includes "put" or "dumped."[4] Perhaps Ishmael was so weakened that he was leaning on his mother for support. When they came to the bush, she allowed his limp body to collapse into the small patch of shade.

Hagar then moved far enough away to avoid watching her son die of thirst. The narrator informed us that she chose a spot "about a bowshot away" (21:6), about two hundred yards. Imagine her dilemma. She no doubt wanted to be with her son to comfort him while he was dying, but she could not bear to watch. What a deeply tragic scene: two people dying, out of sight and earshot of each other. This picture, however tragic, captures the alienation experienced by humanity because of sin. Humans, created to live together in harmony, dying alone. Humans, created to steward creation toward its divinely designed destiny, dying at the hands of unfeeling nature.

Into this sin-cursed scene came a message from the God who hears the cries of outcasts (21:17–19). Both Hagar and her son were crying, but it was Ishmael's cries to which God responded. It makes sense that God would hear the boy he had named "God hears," but it is also worth noting that God compassionately hears our cries, even when those closest to us can no longer bear to listen. As well, specifying that God heard Ishmael may be yet another way of demonstrating the importance of Abraham's son, that is, the importance of Abraham.

Although God heard the boy, he sent an angel to speak to the mother. She still had a job to do on her son's behalf. This helps explain the question he asked a dying woman: "What is the matter, Hagar?" (21:17). God already knew who she was and that her situation was not hopeless, as she assumed. Realizing God knows us and we still have reason to hope is comforting news. The angel told Hagar she was not to fear, because "God heard the boy crying" (21:17). Not only did God know about Hagar, he also knew about her son.

The angel then gave Hagar her assignment. She was to "lift the boy up and take him by the hand" (21:18). More than a command to help him get up, she was being told to "hold him safe" (NJB) or "comfort him" (NLT). Ishmael would not die of thirst beneath a bush in the desert but enjoy a great destiny. Earlier, God had told her Ishmael would have many descendants (16:10), but now she learned that God would "make him into a great nation" (21:18).

Partly to provide for their needs but also to highlight her responsibility to shepherd him to his destiny, God opened Hagar's eyes to see the nearby well (21:19). She took a goatskin, filled it with water from the well, and gave the water to Ishmael. We do not know why she had not seen this well before. Perhaps God had kept her from seeing it. Perhaps she had been unable to see this well because of her poor physical condition or because it lay just out of sight.

Revived, Hagar and Ishmael continued on their journey, not to Egypt but to the "Desert of Paran" (21:21) that lay between Canaan and Sinai. She did not return to her own country but did find an Egyptian girl for her son to marry. God was with the boy and kept his promise to bring from him a great nation (25:12–18). Later conflicts between Isaac's and Ishmael's descendants should not be read back into the biblical account. Although not the child of the promise, Ishmael remained a recipient of God's favor as a child of Abraham.

TREATY AT BEERSHEBA (GEN. 21:22–34)

The narrator introduced this apparently unrelated episode as occurring "at that time" (21:22), that is, around the same time as Hagar and Ishmael's departure. Some contend that Abimelek and Phicol were invited to the great feast mentioned in verse 8 and made their proposition then, but this seems unlikely. The encounter between Abraham and Abimelek took place at Beersheba (21:32), the same region where Hagar saw the well. Hagar had wandered for some time after leaving Abraham's camp before arriving at Beersheba, suggesting she had traveled some distance. More likely, when Abraham became aware of the events described in verses 14–19, he traveled to the well at Beersheba where Hagar and Ishmael had encountered God. It was here that Abraham met the Philistine leaders.

It could be that the only connection between these two stories is that they both occurred in Beersheba, but this seems unlikely. The narrator showed great skill in crafting the narrative of Abraham's life and, as we will see, employed that skill in this brief episode.

We read about Abimelek in the previous chapter, when Abraham's deception nearly cost the king his country. Abimelek had encouraged Abraham to remain in the land, and the patriarch had taken him up on his offer. During Abraham's stay among the Philistines, Abimelek had ample opportunity to witness God's blessing on Abraham's life (see 20:7). The king reasoned that Abraham was the kind of person he wanted on his side, so he decided to formalize their good relationship by making a treaty or covenant.

The narrator carefully constructed this story by interweaving his description of the covenant ceremony with a specific complaint Abraham had against Abimelek.

- Agreement to swear a treaty (21:22–24).
- Abraham's complaint voiced (21:25–26).
- Abraham's offering for the treaty (21:27, 31).
- Abraham's complaint resolved (21:28–30).

One effect of this arrangement is that it highlights Abraham's wisdom in the face of potential conflict. He knew how to work with people, even powerful ones. In Abimelek's words—"God is with you in everything you do" (21:22)—we see that God was keeping his promise to bless Abraham. Abimelek was impressed. On top of vast holdings of flocks, herds, and servants, Abraham had fathered a son in his old age from a wife who was both old and barren. Similar observations of God's blessing would be made later regarding Abraham (23:6) and other figures in the covenant line: Isaac (26:28), Jacob (30:27), and Joseph (39:3).

Abimelek wanted Abraham to enter into a treaty of mutual nonaggression that would be in effect not only during their lifetime, but also for succeeding generations (21:23). The king's specific reference to deceit (21:23) might imply some suspicion of Abraham in light of earlier events. Abimelek also mentioned his past kindness to the patriarch, perhaps a way of reminding Abraham that some of these sheep, cattle, and servants had come from him (20:14).

Abraham expressed his willingness to be Abimelek's covenant partner before exercising one of the privileges of such an agreement, the voicing of a complaint (21:25–26). Abimelek's servants had seized a well to which Abraham felt he had a legal claim. Perhaps his servants had dug the well. Some have suggested, based on the Hebrew verb used, that this was not the first time Abraham had made this complaint to Abimelek's men. The king claimed to know nothing about any such seizure. Given his deep respect for Abraham—respect bordering on fear—we should probably take him at his word. Abraham did not argue with the king. Instead, he allowed his actions to speak.

Our attention is now directed back to the treaty (21:27). Abraham brought his animals, and the king possibly added his own. The two men then cut a deal by dividing the animals in half and walking between the pieces in a way similar to the ceremony described in Genesis 15. When Abimelek noticed the seven additional lambs, he inquired about their purpose. Abraham explained they were intended to assure Abimelek that the well in question did in fact belong to him (21:30). The lambs might have been a tangible demonstration of Abraham's sincerity or payment for the well. This was the first piece of territory Abraham owned in the land that would one day belong to his descendants.

The well came to be known as Beersheba, a name that could mean "well of seven" or "well of the oath" (21:31). Arguments have been raised for each possibility, but it may be that the name was chosen precisely for its clever ambiguity. It reflected both the treaty and dispute about the ownership of the well, and both plot lines are interwoven in the telling of the story.

The closing verses of this chapter describe how Abraham settled in the territory around Beersheba. He spent a considerable amount of time there as did his son Isaac. After Abimelek and Phicol returned to Gerar, Abraham planted a tamarisk tree (21:33). This kind of tree grows well in arid regions. It reaches heights of thirty feet and requires little water because it sends down deep roots. Nomads used tamarisks for shade and food for their flocks. By planting this tree, Abraham demonstrated his intention to remain at Beersheba longer than a season or two. Some have suggested that the tree was intended for the same purpose as the altars built earlier—to commemorate significant events.

What event did Abraham want to commemorate? It might have been the treaty with Abimelek or the purchase of territory in Canaan, but an even more significant event was God's encounter with Hagar, sparing the life of Ishmael and his mother. This might explain why Abraham chose to plant a tree rather than build an altar. When Hagar wanted to place her dying son in the shade, all she could find was a bush. Now, there was a large spreading tree that offered abundant shade to all who passed by. The connection between these stories is not random. This was a place where God showed his kindness and Abraham responded with a tangible demonstration of his faith.

After Abimelek left, Abraham "called on the name of the LORD, the Eternal God" (21:33). He had called on God twice before when he camped near Bethel (12:8; 13:4). As discussed earlier in connection with those passages, the phrase "called on the name of the LORD" could refer to prayer, worship, or some form of proclamation. Since Abraham chose this moment to name God, it seems the last option fits best. Abraham proclaimed to those who would listen that Yahweh, his God, was the eternal God.

Given what Abraham had experienced, this seems an especially appropriate name for God. The long-awaited child had finally arrived. Twenty-five years of waiting must have felt like an eternity to Abraham and Sarah, but God had finally kept his word. Isaac's birth was the most dramatic example of God's faithfulness to date, but Genesis 21 contains other evidence of this divine characteristic as well. By rescuing Hagar and Ishmael, God kept his promise to preserve Abraham's other son. Abimelek's acknowledgment that God had blessed Abraham's life testified that God was remaining faithful to his promise.

Calling God "eternal" was also Abraham's way of affirming that God would keep his promises in spite of pressing challenges. Sarah's barrenness, Lot's unwise choices, a powerful coalition of enemies, Abraham's own lapses into fear, the conflict that rocked Abraham's household, and the unsparing heat of the Beersheba wilderness all stood in the way of God fulfilling his word. But an eternal God is undeterred by time and circumstances. This truth about God serves as a shelter even more enduring than a tamarisk tree.

CONCLUSION

By publicly proclaiming Yahweh as the eternal God, Abraham testified to his conviction that God could be trusted for whatever the future might hold. He also announced his intention to follow this eternal God no matter what the future might bring. Little did he know that he would need every ounce of that faith for the test that lay close ahead.

No Other Gods

GENESIS 22

If Genesis 17 marks a watershed moment in God's dealings with Abraham, then Genesis 22 documents the climax of the patriarch's walk of faith. Few stories in the Bible are more compelling than the account of Abraham's sacrifice of Isaac. The narrator described it as a test, and so it was. Abraham was being tested to determine his deepest loyalties. God was being tested too, for he had demanded Isaac's death when all his promises depended on Isaac staying alive. We are also being tested as we read this story. What will we do when we realize that God asks us to surrender what matters most to us?

ABRAHAM WAS TESTED (GEN. 22:1–19)
····◆····

While encamped near Beersheba, Abraham heard from God. Previous divine visits had brought divine promises, and the plan was unfolding as promised; all that remained now was for Isaac to grow up, get married, and have children of his own. Nothing could have prepared Abraham for what God would ask of him. "Take your son, your only son, whom you love—Isaac—and go to the region of Moriah. Sacrifice him there as a burnt offering on a mountain I will show you" (22:2). The narrator told us this was a test (22:1). God intended to test Abraham by passing him through a fire of unspeakable difficulty. God already knew how this test would turn out. Isaac would be spared, and it would become a crucial moment in preparing the father of all believers. Abraham, however, was completely in the dark. Moments before, everything had made sense and had been predictable. Now all was as black as a starless, moonless night in the desert. God had not just extinguished the light, but had done so with painful clarity. He began with chilling politeness—the command may also be translated "Please take"—letting Abraham know this was not a punishment and God was perfectly aware of what he was demanding.[1] He worded his command precisely, leaving no room for misunderstanding—"your son, your only son." Abraham had another son, Ishmael, but God had allowed him to depart, much to Abraham's deep paternal sorrow. The one son who remained and was deeply loved by his parents was the son God indicated. As if there were some question, God then specified the son by name, Isaac. This boy, whose name means laughter, whose birth had been the subject of multiple predictions, each greeted with incredulous smirks, whose birth had caused the household to erupt in gales of laughter, through whom God had promised to continue Abraham's line, *this* was the son God demanded.

Abraham and Isaac were to travel to the region of Moriah. The journey would take three days. This distance, too, seems to have been part of the test for Abraham. He must not only go, but continue the journey while a million excuses clutched at his robe. Once he and Isaac arrived at the specified mountain, Abraham was to sacrifice Isaac as a "burnt offering" (22:2). This type of sacrifice meant that

Abraham must kill Isaac and burn his body to indicate Abraham's wholehearted devotion to God.

The content and cadence of this horrific command was intended to remind Abraham that God had commanded him to leave his country, people, and father's household and go where he was directed (12:1). Abraham could not miss the irony that the command that forged his destiny was echoed in the command that eliminated every shred of hope.

Abraham never questioned God. What God demanded violated human sentiment, contradicted common sense, negated multiple divine promises, and erased all Abraham's ambitions. Would the man who negotiated for Sodom (18:16–33) and appealed for Ishmael (17:18–20) agree to this demand without a whimper of protest? Abraham said nothing. Perhaps the politeness and crystal clarity of God's command had signaled the futility of debate.[2]

This test was meant to determine who Abraham would ultimately trust. Would it be God or the rivals who were beginning to assert themselves? The temptation to place faith in something other than God is an inescapable aspect of human life in a fallen world. The circumstances of his life would have made Abraham especially vulnerable to such temptations. Abraham was not tempted to worship the idols of his ancestors or of the Canaanites, yet he still faced the temptation to be idolatrous—to worship the very things God had given him instead of the God who gave them.

Many parent understands how easily children can rival God for our loyalty. Although parent-child relationships differ from culture to culture, Abraham and Sarah would have found it difficult not to idolize Isaac. They had waited for him for a long time and had received him in a miraculous fashion. Everything rested on him. He was the crucial link between the elderly couple and the blessings God had promised.

Abraham also faced the temptation to idolize his own success. His résumé was enviable. God had selected him. He had maintained his faith through decades of waiting and had finally received what God had promised. Those who are most blessed are also most vulnerable to pride. As Paul cautioned, those who think they are standing firm should be careful not to fall (1 Cor. 10:12).

Because God had summoned Abraham to be the pioneer of his redemptive plan, Abraham was particularly vulnerable to idolizing the plan itself. Prior to Isaac's birth, this temptation would have been weaker because the birth could be accomplished only by a miracle. With Isaac's arrival, Abraham would have been tempted to assume he knew how things would proceed from this point. The predictable progression of the plan was in danger of shifting from being his destiny to being his possession.

We could not live in this world without its predictability. We can assume the sun will rise in the morning because it always does. We can assume our supper will nourish us rather than poison us because that is what always happens. Predictability is a wonderful gift, but it can also become an idol. We can come to trust the laws of cause and effect more than the God who established those laws. When the unpredictable occurs, we panic, much as Abraham did when he moved into foreign territory (see Gen. 12:10–20; 20:1–18). To protect Abraham from idolizing the plan, God needed to remind him that God's plan without God's presence would no longer be God's plan. God is able to be faithful without being predictable. He can, as someone has said, draw straight with crooked lines.

As if these idols were not tempting enough, at least one more thing clamored for Abraham's loyalty: his understanding of God. It might seem strange to think of one's image of God as a possible idol, but it can easily become that. When we gravitate toward a certain picture of God as we see him in the Bible and in our experience, we may refuse to accept any challenge to that picture that arises from another person's experience or from the Bible itself. When that happens, we have made an idol of our understanding. If we came to faith in an emotionally charged moment and cannot imagine God working through quiet rituals, we are in danger. If our experience of God is mostly one of daily companionship and we react suspiciously to a God of signs and wonders, we are in danger. If we have known much of God's comforting presence, we may greet his silence with disbelief.

Earlier, Abraham had shown himself resistant to this temptation. When he discovered from Melchizedek that Yahweh had other worshipers, he immediately embraced this truth (14:18–22). Regarding Sodom, he discovered he could reason with God (18:16–33). From Abimelek, he learned God's light could shine where it seemed impossible (ch. 20). However, those who have had profound encounters with God are especially vulnerable to this temptation. Experiences like these leave such a deep impression that all new possibilities tend to run into the same groove.

The Jews of the first century gravitated toward a picture of God as powerful. They could support their picture with numerous passages from Scripture. What they could not see, however, was that this powerful God was also willing to make himself weak in the person of Jesus. We are right to worship God as loving but wrong to define God's love in such a way that no room remains for his beloved to suffer. We are right to worship God as just but wrong to understand divine justice as having to occur by our timetable and criteria. God is faithful but not predictable. We must resist the temptation to worship an image of God rather than God as he really is. God tolerates no rivals, not even when they resemble him.

"Early the next morning" (22:3), Abraham began getting ready for his journey, suggesting the immediacy of his obedience. If there ever was a morning Abraham was tempted to sleep in, this was surely it. Instead, he arose early to prepare. His steely resolve had not developed overnight; it had been forged through decades of delay, his failures, and his love for and loss of Ishmael. All these challenges had strengthened the muscle of his faith in preparation for this herculean effort.

Abraham went about his preparations in unusual order. We might have expected him to cut the wood first and saddle his donkey last (22:3). The disorder may reflect Abraham's distracted mind, but more likely his actions were deliberate. By first saddling his donkey he cemented his intention. By waiting to gather wood until just before leaving, he limited others' suspicions. By bringing his own firewood rather than waiting until he arrived at Moriah, he ensured he could carry out God's directive without delay.

Abraham arrived at the region of Moriah on the third day. At the foot of the divinely appointed mountain, Abraham left the donkey with servants, assuring them that he and the boy would return. It is possible that Abraham was being disingenuous, but this seems unlikely. He had no reason to lie to his servants. Further, he believed God would resuscitate Isaac after the sacrifice (see Heb. 11:17–19), so they would both return.

Why then did Abraham choose to leave behind his donkey and servants? One commentator suggests he left the donkey behind to delay his journey to the place of sacrifice, although this would contradict his earlier promptness.[3] Other commentators believe the servants were left behind so they could not impede Abraham's plans, but it seems doubtful that any servants would be so bold.

More likely, he left the donkey and servants behind to spare them the agony of witnessing the horrible event that was about to occur. Yes, Abraham believed he would receive Isaac back alive, but he would still have to kill his son. No one, including the servants, should have to witness such horror.

There may be yet another reason why Abraham left the servants and the donkey behind. Without their help, someone had to carry the wood. Abraham's hands were already full "with the fire" (likely a fire pot such as we saw in 15:17) "and the knife" (22:6). This left only Isaac. By requiring his son to carry the wood, Abraham permitted Isaac to embrace his destiny as God's servant, becoming "obedient to death" (Phil. 2:8). Christians have long recognized the similarity between Isaac carrying the wood for his own sacrifice and Christ carrying his cross to Calvary (see John 19:17). An early Christian hymn speaks of "Isaac, who as a slave bare the image of the King his Master on his shoulders, even the sign of his cross."[4]

The sight of father and son together moving resolutely toward this crucial moment in God's plan beautifully illustrates the words of the prophet Isaiah: "He was led like a lamb to the slaughter, and as a sheep before its shearers is silent, so he did not open his mouth. . . . Yet it was the LORD's will to crush him and cause him to suffer, and though the LORD makes his life an offering for sin, he will see his offspring and prolong his days, and the will of the LORD will prosper in his hand" (Isa. 53:7, 10).

As they walked up the mountain, Isaac asked, "Where is the lamb for the burnt offering?" (Gen. 22:7). He likely knew what was about to happen. Child sacrifices were not unknown at this time, and Isaac also knew the firstborn son was the preferred child for the sacrifice (see 2 Kings 3:27). He had held this status since Ishmael's departure. Furthermore, Isaac had watched his father carefully prepare for the offering. Abraham had remembered everything else, so the absence of the lamb must have been intentional. With his question, Isaac sought to confirm what he strongly suspected: he was to be the sacrificial lamb. Perhaps there was also a humble appeal in his question, as if imploring his father to find some other way. He would not be the last son to ask a father to "let this cup pass" from him.

Abraham's reply was intentionally ambiguous: "God himself will provide the lamb for the burnt offering, my son" (Gen. 22:8). Perhaps he was ambiguous because he could not bring himself to tell Isaac the whole truth. More likely his answer reflects the ambiguity that characterizes mature faith. He did not know exactly what would happen on the mountain, nor how God would reconcile his earlier promises with this most recent command. What Abraham knew was that he could depend on God to provide all that was needed. Whatever God had promised, he would fulfill.

Abraham did not say, "God will provide for us," but "God himself will provide." The patriarch understood that the responsibility to reconcile the divine promises with this command did not rest with him, but with the One who made those promises. Abraham knew God was putting his own faithfulness to the test. Faith is not easy; few passages make this point more clearly, but in moments like these, we need to remember that the One we trust does the heavy lifting. Faith is maintaining our confidence in God and demonstrating that confidence by obedience.

Abraham did not know how God would prove to be reliable, but he continued to believe that he was reliable. Abraham did not try to make God's ways understandable. He did not demand a divine explanation before believing. Nor did he hold God hostage to his limited understanding. Instead, he believed "God's method was his own affair."[5]

Abraham did not deceive Isaac by making the situation less serious than it was, nor did he take the burden off God. The Danish philosopher Søren Kierkegaard suggests Abraham told Isaac this was all his idea, not God's. "Better is it that he believes me inhuman," Abraham prayed, "than that he should lose his faith in thee."[6]

Abraham asserted what he knew to be true, that God would provide (22:8). In the preceding decades, Abraham had learned that no one can predict what God will do based on present circumstances. A more reliable predictor is God's character, as proven by his past deeds. God had always provided, though in unpredictable and inexplicable ways. The present paradox between promise and command was less of a problem because of God's proven nature as provider.

In this life we will never escape the paradox between what is promised and what we experience. We must not slip into easy explanations that ignore the tension by making God seem understandable and safe. We must not think we can explain away the paradox, replacing the God of the Bible with one who fits into our plans, a pocket-sized, portable idol. Nor should we consign all God's doings to the mysterious. Doing so creates a false division of labor between divine and human realms, God being relegated to his department, while we go about the business of living. To believe in the God of the Bible, we must retain the tension between a God whose ways are inscrutable yet is faithful to keep his promises. We must confess with absolute certainty what we cannot fully comprehend. "We pay him the highest honour," wrote Calvin, "when, in affairs of perplexity, we nevertheless entirely acquiesce in his providence."[7]

When they reached the appointed spot, Abraham began to prepare for the sacrifice by building the altar and arranging the wood. We do not know what Isaac was doing at this time, but he probably worked alongside his father, helping find suitable rocks and handing him pieces of wood. When all was ready, Abraham turned to Isaac and "bound" him (22:9). That Abraham was able to bind his son and lay him on the altar suggests Isaac offered himself as a willing sacrifice. If he had wanted to resist, there was little his aged father could have done to prevent him. Isaac's deep reverence for God, even to the point of voluntarily surrendering his life in obedience to God's command, helps explain one of the most unusual names for God found in the Old Testament: "Fear of Isaac" (31:42, 53). His willing obedience, even to the point of death, made Isaac a model for generations of believers. "Isaac feared the Lord," wrote the early church father, Ambrose, "as was indeed but natural in the son of Abraham; being subject also to his father to such an extent that he would not avoid death in opposition to his father's will."[8]

The narrator slowed the action so we clearly see each movement: the stretching out of Abraham's hand and the grasping of the hilt of the knife (22:10). Before Abraham was able to strike the fatal blow, perhaps even before he was able to lift the knife, an angel interrupted Abraham's hard obedience with a voice from heaven. The phrase, "from heaven" (22:11), while not strictly necessary, may clarify that the angel did not appear physically. Had he done so, Abraham might have mistaken him for a human and proceeded with the sacrifice.

For the third time in the story, Abraham responded with *hinneh*, which means "Here I am" or "I'm listening." The first time was in response to God's initial command, the second to Isaac's only comment during this journey, and this time to the angel calling his name. Each marks an important moment in the story: the command, Isaac's veiled appeal, and the end of the test. Abraham's responses were crucial to passing this test: obedience, confidence, obedience. The patriarch could exercise the great faith we see in this story only because he possessed the ability to listen to God and others.

Up to this point in the story, God had been referred to as Elohim (22:1, 3, 8, 9). Only in verse 11 does the name Yahweh appear. The narrator may have used the different names to show how Abraham was coming to understand God more clearly. The perplexity of God demanding back what he had miraculously provided is represented by Elohim, a generic name for God known throughout the ancient Near East. The clarification that this was only a test is symbolized by the use of Yahweh, a name that connotes the fuller revelation God made to Abraham and his descendants.

Twice the angel prohibited Abraham from proceeding with the sacrifice: "Do not lay a hand on the boy. . . . Do not do anything to him" (22:12). The repetition shows how God's heart abhorred child sacrifice. Through unflinching obedience, Abraham had demonstrated his wholehearted fear of God. In the past, Abraham had a problem with fear. On two occasions, he had been so frightened that he had jeopardized God's plan (see 12:10–20; 20:1–18). Abraham's problem was not *that* he feared, but the *object* of his fear. In this terrifying test, he learned that he should fear only God.

Abraham demonstrated his fear of God by not withholding his only son. The repetition, "your son, your only son" (22:1), echoes the initial command and highlights the essence of this test. Abraham was willing to surrender his one and only son and all that Isaac represented. Abraham feared God more than he feared life without Isaac.

The story could have ended here, but it didn't. God had commanded a burnt offering, so a burnt offering was mandatory. Abraham had assumed Isaac would be the sacrificial offering, but God had emphatically prohibited this. What would Abraham offer? Given the opportunity, he might have asked God the same question Isaac had asked him: "Where is the lamb for the burnt offering?" (22:7).

He was not given the chance because God quickly provided. In the bushes behind Abraham was a ram with its horns caught in a thicket. It had probably been there all along, but Abraham had not noticed it in the intensity of the moment. As with Hagar finding the well (see 21:19), Abraham recognized as divine providence what others might call a lucky coincidence. Only people of faith recognize that God has provided.

God's provision of the ram was a lesson to the future Israelites, reinforcing the divine prohibition of human sacrifice and the insistence on animal sacrifices. The Christian can hardly miss the parallels between this incident and Christ's death on the cross. Here was a picture of a substitute provided by God without cost and even before the need was known. Though he possessed thousands of sacrificial animals back home in Beersheba, Abraham had nothing with which to pay the debt he owed on Mount Moriah. Entirely by grace, God provided the needed sacrifice, whose death satisfied divine justice.

Because of the great significance of this moment in his life, Abraham named the spot. The name Abraham chose celebrated God's character, not his own. He called it "The LORD Will Provide" (22:14). This was the perfect name because at this place God had provided the ram in place of Isaac. Even more, God had provided Isaac to Abraham for a second time, the first through Sarah, the second through the fire of testing. There is one surprise in the name, however, because Abraham did not put the verb in the perfect tense (The LORD has provided) but in the imperfect tense, suggesting incomplete or ongoing action. Abraham not only commemorated what God had done, but also announced, based on God's nature, what he would continue to do. This may be why future generations of Abraham's descendants saw this description of God fulfilled in their own time ("to this day," 22:14).

Abraham's choice of verb tense is significant for another reason. The spot where this sacrifice took place, Mount Moriah, was very likely where Solomon later built the temple (see 2 Chron. 3:1). There, too, God would provide for his people, graciously granting forgiveness for sins and allowing them to experience his presence. Even more significant, very near the site of Abraham's test, God would provide another sacrificial offering, "the Lamb of God, who takes away the sin of the world" (John 1:29). "On the mountain of the LORD . . . will be provided" (Gen. 22:14), the fulfillment of God's redemptive plan, humanity's reconciliation to God, itself, others, and nature.

This test was about whether Abraham would trust God or one of the idols vying for God's place in his life. Abraham's response demonstrated the kind of faith God seeks. The patriarch chose to obey God, trusting in his goodness even when God demanded something not at all good, the death of the son for whom Abraham had waited so long and on whom so much depended. When God's demand shattered Abraham's understanding of God, he clung to what he knew in the face of what he could not comprehend. A weaker faith would have disobeyed or delayed. A weaker faith might have obeyed but in despair, refusing to believe there was any hope beyond this mountain of death. A weaker faith might have obeyed bitterly, agreeing to God's demands but refraining from ever fully trusting God again. Abraham's faith enabled him not only to promptly obey, but to hope for a miracle.

Abraham's faith was in God, not in his image of God. We know this because when God asked something that didn't make sense, Abraham expanded his understanding of God to embrace unpredictability as a divine quality. Through this test, Abraham came to realize a truth essential to real faith: We can and must trust God. Even when God seems to have betrayed us, we must continue to believe. We must have faith in the One who appears to have forgotten, even forsaken us.

Abraham's experience of faith provided the prototype for all believers, for this is the only kind of faith that allows us to participate in God's redemptive plan. If we believe only what we can understand, or makes sense to us, God's plan lies beyond our comprehension. We will never accept the eternal God who befriended the elderly Abraham, promised children from barren wombs, compassionately saw those who spent centuries in slavery, and emancipated them through the Red Sea. If we cannot grasp such things, how could we ever believe that God became as an infant who grew up to die a criminal's death and then rose to life again? How could we believe that in Jesus' dying and rising, God's plan of redemption reached its consummation? Unless we accept what we cannot understand, and follow the One we cannot see, we cannot truly believe.

After the sacrifice of the ram, God was still not finished with Abraham. He spoke through the angel a second time, reaffirming his promises in their strongest form yet (22:15–18). Because he can swear by no one more reliable than himself, God swore by himself that he would do all he had promised. This is the first and only time God swore an oath to the patriarchs, thereby establishing a moment to which Abraham and future generations would often return for assurance (see 24:7; 26:3; 50:24; Ex. 13:5).[9] God introduced the reaffirmation of his promises with "declares the LORD" (Gen. 22:16), a phrase that appears often in the prophetic books, but only here in Genesis and one other time in the Pentateuch (Num. 14:28).

Because of what Abraham did on Mount Moriah, God repeated his earlier promises with extra emphasis. The New American Standard Bible captures this emphasis well: "Indeed I will greatly bless you, and I will greatly multiply your seed as the stars of the heavens" (Gen. 22:17). On other occasions, God has used either stars (15:5) or dust (13:16) as an illustration of Abraham's numerous descendants. Here God repeated the star metaphor and added another— grains of sand (22:17). As before, God repeated his promises and added something new: Abraham's descendants would experience military victory (22:17), likely alluding to the conquest of Canaan. So as to leave no doubt about the reason for God's enthusiasm, the angel concluded as he began, with a reference to Abraham's obedience in offering Isaac.

These words, and the spirit with which they were spoken, must have profoundly affected Abraham, given what he had just endured. He would understand more clearly the importance of obeying no matter how incomprehensible God's commands might seem. Any lingering questions about God's goodness or his plan could be brushed aside.

NAHOR'S SONS (GEN. 22:20–24)

Is there any connection between the powerful story of faith in verses 1–19 and the genealogy of Abraham's brother, Nahor? Some say no and note that the narrator often used the phrase "some time later" (22:20) to mark the beginning of a new section. However, there does seem to be a connection between the two passages because both describe how God provided for the furtherance of his redemptive plan. The first demonstrates how God provides in response to faith, while the second anticipates how God will provide for the continuation of Abraham's line by providing a wife for Isaac. Not only will Isaac live on, he will marry a woman who is not a Canaanite, but one of Abraham's own relatives (see 24:1–4).

CONCLUSION

Both Abraham and God passed their tests. The patriarch proved he would allow no idols in God's place. God demonstrated that he will keep his promises, even when he seems to have backed himself into a corner. God provided for Isaac a second time and hinted at how he intended to provide for Isaac in the future. Mount Moriah marks the summit of Abraham's life but not its sunset. He had more challenges to face and more lessons to learn before reaching the good death God had promised.

12

Behind the Scenes

GENESIS 23–25

The big idea of Genesis 22, God's provision, continues to unfold in chapters 23–25 but in a more subtle way. In these closing episodes of Abraham's life, we have no divine appearances or messages. Instead, we watch as things just work out in ways favorable to Abraham. Some might consider these to be lucky breaks or the result of human skill, but those with faith know that God was continuing to provide for the patriarch, albeit behind the scenes.

SARAH'S DEATH AND BURIAL (GEN. 23:1–20)

The most important woman in the Bible since Eve died at the age of 127 (23:1). Sarah spent her first ninety years as a barren woman and the last thirty-seven as the mother of her beloved Isaac. She left the settled life of the city with her husband to become a nomad. Twice she was forced into another man's harem because of her husband's fear. She was partly responsible for the birth of Ishmael and largely to blame for his expulsion from the household. When she was eighty-nine and still barren, God changed her name to emphasize that she would become the mother of nations. Though not perfect, she deserves considerable credit for supporting Abraham during their joint pilgrimage of faith.

When Sarah died at Hebron, Abraham mourned his wife (23:2). The Hebrew verb for *went* can be translated to suggest that Abraham went to her, as if he came from another location where he was perhaps looking after the flocks in the field. Some translators render this verb as "went in" to her (ESV, NRSV, NASB), implying he entered the tent where she had died. Still others treat the verb as part of an idiom for carrying out the mourning customs (NJB). Whichever meaning one chooses, Abraham clearly grieved Sarah's death, likely with loud weeping, torn garments, sackcloth, and fasting.

Then Abraham arose from beside Sarah's body and went to the city gates to negotiate with the elders of Hebron for a burial site (23:3, 18). This was not Abraham's only option. Nomads sometimes transported the remains of their dead until they could bury them elsewhere. Abraham could have taken Sarah's body back to Harran or Ur and buried her with his ancestors. His home, however, was no longer in Mesopotamia but in Canaan, the land Yahweh had promised him. He would bury his wife in a new family tomb in the land he was certain would one day belong to his descendants.

The problem was, as a resident alien (that is "foreigner and stranger," 23:4), he could own no land without the permission of the city elders. So Abraham made his way to the gates of Hebron among the "Hittites" (23:3) or "sons of Heth" (NASB). The latter phrase is possible because a Heth is mentioned in Genesis 10:15, though the New International Version renders it as *Hittite*. One commentator suggests these were Heth's offspring.[1] The Hittites were a people from distant Asia Minor (now central Turkey). Some believe a group of these Hittites migrated south to Canaan's hill country between 1800 and 1200 BC (compare Josh. 11:3).[2] Whoever they were, they would decide whether Abraham could purchase "property for a burial site" (Gen. 23:4). This phrase indicates a piece of land that could become part of one's inheritance. Abraham was looking not only for a place to bury his wife, but also for a piece of land that could be passed down through his family line. He wanted a family burial site that would be used for the centuries to come.

Abraham delivered his request in three parts. He asked the city elders to sell him a piece of land so he could bury Sarah (23:4). The elders responded by giving Abraham the pick of the best of the tombs they had to offer (23:6). Note that they offered him the chance to bury Sarah in one of their tombs, but this was not what he had asked for. He had requested permission to purchase territory.

Although the elders were somewhat resistant, they paid Abraham a significant compliment, calling him a "mighty prince" (23:6). This term, literally means "prince of God" (NJB) and demonstrates their deep admiration. They were affirming what others had observed about Abraham: that he had been blessed by God (see 14:19; 21:22) just as God had promised. Some of this blessing had come from the coffers of Pharaoh and Abimelek, but much had come through Abraham's animal husbandry. So the elders were giving something more than a compliment. They were acknowledging Abraham's status before God. This recognition helps explain why they eventually agreed to Abraham's request.

Having heard their initial reply, Abraham prepared to make his second request. Before making it, this "mighty prince" assumed a posture of great humility. Then he asked the elders to intercede with Ephron, one of their own, so that he would sell—not loan—Abraham a piece of land (23:8–9). Ephron was sitting among the elders, so

Abraham could have asked him directly. The custom of that time (and today in some cultures) was to avoid the possibility of public embarrassment by negotiating through a mediator.

Ephron's offer (23:11) is an excellent example of the kind of negotiating that occurs in many parts of the world today. Less clear is the precise nature of what Ephron offered. Perhaps Ephron's offer to "give" the land was a polite way of referring to a purchase. If so, Ephron agreed to sell property to Abraham, which would mean the patriarch obtained what he had asked for. This seems unlikely because Abraham responded by insisting on paying for the land (23:13). The beginning of Abraham's response is quite strong in the original, and is captured well by the New Living Translation's "No, listen to me," and the New Revised Standard Version's "If you only will listen to me!" Abraham's frustration is best explained by Ephron's refusal to sell. Most likely Ephron was offering to literally give Abraham the field and cave. Abraham did not want this field and cave as a gift because in the culture of the time a gift placed "the recipient under obligation to the donor."[3] If Abraham did not want to be obligated to the king of Sodom (14:22–24), he would not have wanted to be obligated to Ephron either. Even worse, Ephron's heirs could have reclaimed the land after their father's death.

Finally, Ephron agreed to sell both the field and cave. His decision to part with the entire parcel may have had something to do with the pressure he felt from the elders. It may also have had something to do with Hittite law, where the original landowner (in this case, Ephron) would continue to pay dues (similar to real estate taxes) if he sold only a portion of his property. If the entire tract were sold, the dues became the responsibility of the new landowner, Abraham.

Ephron's price of four hundred shekels (23:14–15) may have been fair, or he may have been gouging the grieving widower; we do not have enough information to know. The price did not matter to Abraham. He was not just buying a piece of property, he was placing a down payment on land that would one day belong to his descendants. Verses 16–17 emphasize that the sale was legally transacted, an important detail given the great significance of this purchase. With it, Abraham honored his wife with a worthy memorial and purchased the family burial site that would be used for generations. He also ceased to be a resident alien in this land and moved one step closer to being its owner.

Even more significant, this purchase brought God's redemptive plan a step closer to fulfillment. The pioneer of the plan had secured the first tract of land for God's covenant people. As promised, God had blessed Abraham so that he gained favor in the eyes of the Hittites and gave the resources to secure this property. Abraham had carefully and resolutely stewarded those resources through negotiations until reaching a successful conclusion. We have seen this divine-human synergy before in Abraham's life (18:16–21) and will witness it in the next episode as well: God's subtle provision joined with faithful obedience from God's people.

ABRAHAM SECURED A WIFE FOR ISAAC (GEN. 24:1–67)

Once again the narrator informed us that Abraham had been richly blessed (24:1), evidence that God's plan was being fulfilled. In order for the plan to continue, however, something was needed besides Abraham's wealth and a burial plot. Isaac needed a wife who would bear children to continue Abraham's line and she could not be Canaanite. Abraham needed to secure a wife from his extended family in Mesopotamia.

There were at least two reasons for Abraham's insistence that Isaac not marry a Canaanite. First, he was well acquainted with Canaanite immorality, having witnessed its debauching effects on his nephew. Second, Abraham likely feared that such a marriage would eventuate his family being assimilated into the Canaanites.

Because Abraham was unable or unwilling to make the journey, he chose to send one of his most trusted servants. Although the Hebrew could be translated "oldest servant," the correct translation is probably "senior servant" (24:2). This would be a hard trip for an old man, and the following phrase specifies this servant as being "in charge of all that [Abraham] had" (24:2). Someone else would need to look after household affairs while more important matters were attended to.

Given his advanced age, Abraham did not know if he would live to meet the woman Isaac would marry. The right choice was crucial, so Abraham could trust only his top man. Even then the servant would need to swear an oath by Yahweh, "the God of heaven and the God of earth" (24:3). Swearing by this expanded divine title would have alerted the servant to the seriousness of his task. Even more, it would have reminded him that Yahweh's authority extended to all the earth and even to heaven itself. Wherever the servant must go to find the right wife for Isaac, God ruled there also. Whatever arrangements would need to be made to find this woman, God could make them from his throne in heaven. The wording "I want you to swear" (24:3) does not fully capture Abraham's seriousness; the New American Standard Bible comes closer to the original with "I will make you swear."

Abraham instructed his servant to return to Mesopotamia ("my country") and find a wife from among the patriarch's "own relatives" (24:4). The servant was not concerned about finding Abraham's town and family. But what if the woman he found would not return to Canaan? "Shall I then take your son back to the country you came from?" (24:5). Although translators are right to treat this as a question, the Hebrew leaves unclear whether the question implies a negative answer ("You don't want me to take him back there, do you?") or a positive one ("Then I should take him back there, right?").

Abraham's answer left no doubt. In the strongest possible terms he forbade the servant from taking Isaac back to Mesopotamia and warned him of dire consequences should he do so. "Make sure" (24:6) is a rendering of a Hebrew idiom meaning "take care" or "beware," a phrase often used to refute a "shocking or unworthy idea."[4] Abraham did not explain why he did not want Isaac to return to Mesopotamia, but we can assume it was because he might forget the covenant and thereby forfeit Canaan. Abraham was confident it would not come to that, for God had sworn to provide many descendants for Abraham. This was the oath God swore on Mount Moriah, just after the cancelled sacrifice of Isaac (22:16–17). We do not know whether Abraham had received the assurance of angelic assistance or just assumed such would be forthcoming, given God's solemn promise. Once more Abraham insisted that, whatever might happen, Isaac must not return to Mesopotamia (24:8).

As directed, the servant swore this oath by promising with his hand beneath Abraham's thigh. This gesture physically reinforced the promise. Joseph would later do the same when he made a promise to his father (47:29).

How fitting that these are Abraham's last recorded words. With them he demonstrated his conviction that God had called and directed his life. With them he affirmed his resolute belief that God would keep his promises. With these words, he proved his commitment and determination to continue God's plan and his insistence that all be done as it should be with no compromises.

The importance of what happened next (24:10–67) can be seen in the detail with which the events are described. The servant obediently traveled to Abraham's homeland, a journey that took about a month.[5] He arrived at the city well when the women were coming to draw water. There he prayed for God's blessing on his efforts as a demonstration of divine "kindness" to his master (24:12). This Hebrew term for kindness, *chesed*, implies a covenant relationship, such as God established with Abraham and reaffirmed several times in the succeeding decades. The servant was asking for more than kindness; he was calling upon God to keep his gracious promises to Abraham.

The servant asked God to provide a sign to indicate the right girl for Isaac: the one who would agree to give him a drink and then offer to water his ten camels would be Miss Right (24:14). This was no arbitrary trial, for the girl would be demonstrating the very qualities one would want in a partner: generosity, hard work, and compassion. Presumably, the servant was prepared to try this with several girls until he found the right one, but God sent Rebekah immediately, even "before he had finished praying" (24:15).

We have read Rebekah's name before, in the brief genealogy that followed the offering of Isaac (22:23). The extended parenthetical note given here (24:15) provides the reader (but not the servant) with very important information: This was a very close relative of Abraham, the granddaughter of his brother. So Rebekah was Isaac's cousin. Rebekah's grandmother, Milkah, was the daughter of Abraham's brother, Haran. After Haran's death, Milkah had become a wife of Abraham's other brother, Nahor. She had borne to him Bethuel, Rebekah's father. Rebekah was related to Abraham in two ways.[6] He had wanted someone from his family, but this was even more than he could have hoped for.

The narrator also informed us that Rebekah was a beautiful virgin. The servant immediately noticed the first of these qualities, and perhaps the second as well. It was customary for virgins in that culture to distinguish themselves in some visible way, for example with a particular veil, dress, or hairstyle. Or Rebekah's virginity may be another detail provided to the reader that the servant learned only later.

According to verse 18, Rebekah gave the servant a drink in response to his request, and she did so humbly, addressing him as "my lord," and quickly, showing both compassion and strength. The narrator masterfully allowed the suspense to build while the servant drank. Now comes the most important question: Would she offer to water the camels? She offered not only to water them, but to give them their fill and continued to move with haste (24:19–20). If she had offered to do this, why then did the servant continue to watch her intently? He was waiting to see if she would follow through on what she promised. After all, she had embarked on no small task. Following a journey, ten camels would require a total of about 250 gallons of water.[7] Each gallon weighs about eight pounds, not counting the pot. She had committed herself to lugging more than a ton of water up and down the steps of the well.

When the camels had slurped their last and were satisfied, the servant was sure he had found the right woman. In his exuberance, he lavished her with expensive jewelry before stopping to ask two important questions: Who was her family, and could he lodge with them (24:23)? Asking the two questions in rapid succession demonstrated both his eagerness and his awareness that God had blessed his journey. When he discovered that Miss Right was also Isaac's cousin, he burst into praise to Yahweh, who had indeed demonstrated kindness (*chesed*) and faithfulness to Abraham by leading him directly to his "master's relatives" (24:26–27).

Meanwhile, Rebekah ran back to her mother's household. If her mother was only one of Bethuel's wives, this would explain why the negotiations were mostly between the servant and Rebekah's mother and Laban (24:29–53). Her father, Bethuel, made only a cameo appearance (24:50).

Here we meet Laban for the first, but not the last, time. He would play a prominent role in the life of Rebekah's son, Jacob. His apparent interest in Abraham's wealth (24:30) may suggest the presence of the less savory character traits that emerged more clearly in Laban's later dealings with his nephew (chs. 29–31).

Custom required Abraham's servant to eat a meal before explaining his mission, but some things could not wait. He began by describing Abraham's great wealth, all of which would go to his heir, a young man born in his mother's old age (24:33–36). Mention of this last detail implies both the blessed circumstances of the boy's birth and that this heir was still relatively young. The servant explained he had come to find a wife for the heir from among Abraham's family, someone who would be willing to live in Canaan. To offset the challenges of such a mission, the servant had been given the promise of divine assistance. Now that God has kept his promise and led him straight to Rebekah, he must have known, even before eating, that the relatives would be willing to arrange a marriage. Since no one could argue that this marriage had all the signs of divine blessing, the family agreed. The servant once again praised Yahweh, then distributed lavish gifts on Rebekah and her family—likely the bride price. Only then did everyone eat the meal.

The next day Rebekah's mother and brother attempted to delay Rebekah's departure, for "ten days or so" (24:55). Some believe the requested delay was for as long as a year.[8] However, the servant was eager to reach home while his master was still alive, and Rebekah was willing to leave immediately, so the caravan began its return journey the day after it had arrived (24:54–61). The parting blessing that spoke of many descendants and triumph over enemies closely echoed God's promise in Genesis 22:16–17. This was one more indication of divine blessing on this journey. God had provided the perfect wife for Isaac through the faith-filled and obedient efforts of Abraham and his servant.

ABRAHAM'S OFFSPRING AND DEATH
(GEN. 25:1–18)

In Genesis 25, we learn of Abraham's death, but the news is tucked in the midst of three other passages, all describing his descendants. By arranging the material this way, the narrator emphasized what one commentator calls "the onward thrust of Genesis."[9] Abraham's death would not be the end. God had promised that because of Abraham's faith and obedience his line would continue, branching into nations and descendants too numerous to count. As is often experienced at the funerals of great saints, we grieve Abraham's passing even while we celebrate what God has provided through him.

At some point, Abraham took another wife in addition to Sarah and Hagar (25:1–6). The marriage may not have taken place until after Sarah died, which could be suggested by the placement of this account. More likely, this marriage occurred earlier, since Keturah is called a concubine rather than a wife. We learn the names of the sons of this marriage and the genealogies of two of these sons, Jokshan and Midian. Abraham gave gifts to his sons but sent them away from Isaac, his sole heir. Although they could have been useful allies to Isaac, Abraham felt it more important that they leave Canaan. This land belonged to the line that passed through Isaac and to that line alone. For God's redemptive plan to be accomplished, Abraham had to send Keturah's sons away. God's plan also called for their eventual return (see Isa. 60:6) because the gospel extends to all nations. The sons were sent away "that there might be a true home, in the end, to return to."[10]

Abraham died at the age of 175 (Gen. 25:7–11). The narrator employed several phrases to describe this death, saying, "Abraham breathed his last and died at a good old age, an old man and full of years; and he was gathered to his people" (25:8). The accumulation of descriptors makes clear that Abraham's death was a good death, an important conclusion to a blessed life. Even in this brief obituary, we clearly see that God had provided everything he promised for this pioneer of the faith.

The firstborn, Ishmael, and the heir, Isaac, buried their father in the cave of Machpelah, where Sarah had been buried decades earlier. The narrator repeated that this was Abraham's property, secured by divine blessing through human faith and obedience. This theme continues in verse 11, where we read of God's blessing on Isaac. The next stage of the plan was already underway.

Another genealogical account follows, this one concerning Ishmael's line (25:12–18). As God had promised, Hagar's son had become the father of twelve sons, each one the head of a tribe. They lived as nomads in "settlements and camps" rather than cities (26:16).

CONCLUSION

As the story of Abraham draws to a conclusion, God remains active but less directly. There are no visions, no dramatic encounters, no divine messages, not even an angel, but God was still providing, and still keeping his promises. Even those who worshiped other gods, such as the Hittites (23:6) and Laban and Bethuel (24:50), testify to this fact. God's blessing is seen in Abraham's good death (25:8) and in how his descendants continue to flourish (25:1–6; 12–18). Divine faithfulness is an important theme in these chapters. Of the six times the term *faithful* (*emet*) is used in Genesis, three are in Genesis 24. God is faithful, though invisible.

Human actions, on the other hand, become more prominent. Abraham had to negotiate for the burial plot, making the purchase with resources provided by God. Abraham had to put his trust in a servant whose quest for Isaac's wife has its own challenges. Those who accomplished God's purposes in these episodes must have been people of faith, willing to step out in the dark. As Walter Brueggemann observes, "We do not always know the gifts of God in advance. But given a perspective of faith, we can in subsequent reflection discern the amazing movement of God in events we had not noticed or which we had assigned to other causes."[11]

The people God uses are those who will obey. Whether that obedience takes them to Hebron's city gate to negotiate for land and a new status or to far-off Nahor to find just the right bride, those employed by this faithful God do what they are supposed to do. "The faith offered here," notes Brueggemann, "is for those willing to be led."[12]

Afterword

※

In Abraham, God's friend, we have discovered how we, too, can become God's friends by faith. We do not send him a friend request on Facebook or earn his friendship by our good deeds. God must graciously choose us, and we must follow with obedient faith. The path may be long and circuitous, but we must continue to follow. We will encounter great difficulties, but we must not waver in our faith. If we walk by faith, we will become sons and daughters of Abraham, "the father of all who believe" (Rom. 4:11). As our father, Abraham is the pioneer of our faith, the prototype for what the life of faith involves, and our example for how to walk by faith.

PIONEER OF THE FAITH
※

Abraham is our father in the faith. He blazed the trail that eventually led to Christ's cross and empty tomb. Jesus is the author and perfecter of this plan, but Abraham is its pioneer. The implementation of this plan began when God summoned Abraham from Ur and Harran. That eternal, divine promise to bless all nations sounded first in Abraham's ears. Before long, God revealed to the pioneer the need for this plan. Because sin has cursed this world, people find themselves alienated from God, each other, themselves, and the natural world. This alienation is apparent even in the opening chapter of Abraham's life. Only in a fallen world could there be famine. When it struck, Abraham decided to leave Canaan rather than trust or even consult God. This is disappointing but not surprising in a world where all people are alienated from God. While in Egypt, Abraham encountered conflict with Pharaoh, which gave evidence of interpersonal alienation. In consequence, he departed Egypt in shame, further evidence of interpersonal alienation. Even the pioneer of God's plan was infected with the disease of sin. Yet Abraham discovered the antidote, grace, which rescued him from Pharaoh and brought him back to his rightful place.

This plan unfolds through God's loving grace and is experienced by personal faith that cooperates with him. Abraham's efforts to further the plan on his own failed. He tried to produce an heir through Hagar, but God did not punish him for his efforts beyond allowing him to experience the pain and frustration those efforts produced. Abraham's responsibility was not to fulfill the plan, but to obey as God fulfilled it. This obedience included the ritual action of circumcision that became the eternal sign of the covenant. It included his participation with God in the process of determining the destiny of Sodom. Abraham's greatest act of obedience occurred when he offered up his only son at God's direction.

God's grace is seen in other ways throughout the life of Abraham, such as when God revealed himself to a runaway Egyptian slave girl and promised a great future to her son. By grace, God revealed himself even outside the covenant with Abraham, to faithful Melchizedek and to the pagan king Abimelek. God's plan to bless all nations led to the Great Commission, but it began centuries earlier, during Abraham's lifetime.

It requires great faith to follow a God who appears only occasionally, reveals his plan in tiny bits, makes promises then delays their fulfillment, and demands incredible sacrifices. Abraham became the father of all believers precisely by believing. God recognized in our father's faith the evidence of righteousness. In response to Abraham's faith, God began to fulfill his divine promises. He brought about the miraculous birth of Abraham and Sarah's son, Isaac, who was the beginning of descendants too numerous to count. He blessed Abraham materially so that even the pagans noticed his prosperity. He allowed Abraham to obtain a toehold in the land of Canaan and provided a wife for Isaac. Some of God's blessings occurred in dramatic fashion, but most appeared almost naturally so that their divine origin was only evident to those with faith.

As God proceeded to inaugurate his plan through our father Abraham, we gain a glimpse of how this plan would unfold. We learn how Abraham's descendants would be enslaved and then liberated. We learn they would one day possess the land of Canaan, and we get further glimpses, such as Abram's deliverance from Egypt, which anticipates the exodus. In God's appearance during the covenant ceremony of Genesis 15, we see a foreshadowing of the incarnation. The ritual of circumcision, commanded in Genesis 17, anticipates the sacrament of baptism as commanded by Christ (Matt. 28:18–20). On Mount Moriah, we see a foreshadowing of the cross and the resurrection, thereby catching a hint that even then God's plan included a way to bring about full reconciliation with all humanity through Abraham.

While Abraham was pioneering God's redemptive plan, he was introduced to the God behind the plan. Some who had lived earlier, such as Adam, Enoch, and Noah, had discovered some aspects of God's character; but Abraham's experiences provide further knowledge of God's character. The lessons began with Abraham's double calling, first from Ur, then from Harran (Gen. 11:31; 12:4). God first emphasized his sovereign ability to command and his capacity to make promises. Doubtless, Abraham also recognized God's patience in granting him a second chance at obedience, and God's faithfulness in appearing to him numerous times. Abraham also learned God's name, Yahweh.

In his first serious challenge of faith, the famine in Canaan and its aftermath (12:10–20), Abraham discovered that while Yahweh calls, makes promises, and appears, he also disappears and remains silent at times, even at moments when his presence and voice would be especially valuable. God would reinforce this lesson several more times in Abraham's life. In fact, we know of only a handful of times when God spoke to Abraham, and only four times when he appeared to him (12:7; 15:17; 17:1; 18:1).

A "guest lecturer" taught Abraham's next lesson on God's character. From Melchizedek, king of Salem, Abraham learned that the God he knew as Yahweh was known to others as El Elyon, "God Most High, Creator of heaven and earth" (14:22). This encounter reinforced Abraham's understanding that God's sovereignty was based on the fact that he had created everything. That Abraham learned this lesson from Melchizedek showed the patriarch that God was up to something much bigger than he understood.

After Abraham met Melchizedek and refused the king of Sodom's offer, God appeared to him a second time. During this encounter, Abraham learned that God was fully aware of all that had been happening and would reward him for his faith (15:1). Abraham learned that God's sovereignty is held in tension with his desire to be Abraham's partner, even to solemnly commit himself to the patriarch (15:17–21). God spoke to Abram as a friend, but he surrounded this friend with a dreadful darkness. Then God illuminated himself and his plan, as symbolized by the torch, even as he concealed himself, as symbolized by the smoking firepot.

Another "guest lecturer" now appeared on the scene: the runaway Egyptian slave girl, Hagar. God had shown his personal interest in her well-being and that of her unborn son. She responded by naming God, "You are the God who sees me" (16:13). Having heard of this encounter, Abraham would have learned of God's personal interest in his servants, including himself. Equally important was the realization that his God felt a special concern for the weak, the outcast, and the foreigner.

In Genesis 17:1, Yahweh identified himself as God Almighty. Abraham had seen glimpses of God's power up to this point, but more evidence was yet to come. God's self-identification was a claim to sovereignty and a call to faithful loyalty. God asserted his power in Genesis 17 then displayed it by punishing Sodom in Genesis 19. Along with God's power, Abraham observed God's justice, the two qualities that are always kept in tandem (chs. 18–19).

Having walked with Yahweh for decades, Abraham became convinced that his God was unlimited by time, and therefore called upon him as "the LORD, the Eternal God" (21:33). Promises made more than twenty-five years earlier had been fulfilled. God had predicted what would happen to Abraham's offspring in centuries to come. By giving God this name, Abraham demonstrated his conviction that God would be faithful to fulfill all the promises he had made. That conviction was put to the test on Mount Moriah, where Abraham's most challenging lessons would be learned (ch. 22). From that test of faith, Abraham learned that God would be faithful even when it seemed God had utterly abandoned his friend. Yahweh might demand the sacrifice of what Abraham held most precious, but would provide something of even greater value.

Abraham's last recorded reference to God is in Genesis 24:3, where he called him "the LORD, the God of heaven and the God of earth." With this title, Abraham summed up his knowledge of God's sweeping sovereignty, omnipotence, incomprehensibility, and eternality. Yet Abraham considered this God to be so personally involved in human affairs that he would serve as divine matchmaker for Isaac.

God's plan flows naturally from his character. He is sufficiently sovereign to reconcile the alienating effects of sin, yet he solved the problem of sin in a very personal way by taking on human flesh. The essence of the sin problem is alienation, especially alienation from God. In the experiences of Abraham, we are introduced to a God whose very character is self-revealing, who wants to be known. Yet this revelation occurs gradually and remains partial, highlighting the need for faith, without which one cannot please God (Heb. 11:6).

PROTOTYPE OF THE FAITH

Abraham pioneered both God's redemptive plan and served as the archetype for the plan's operation in the human realm. His life is the paradigm for all who experience saving faith; in Abraham we discover the genetic code for friendship with God. This friendship begins with a command to follow God, leaving behind our security and identity in exchange for only promises of blessing. We must take up our cross, said Jesus, or we cannot be his disciples. This call comes not as a result of our search for God, but because he has graciously chosen us. It is all grace, from beginning to end.

Just as Abraham began with more questions than answers, we who believe never embark on the road of faith knowing exactly what lies ahead. If we did, we would be on the wrong road, not the road of faith. We must learn to walk in the light as God gives the light, understanding more as God reveals it. At times we learn directly from God. At other times we learn from others and our own experiences.

The walk of faith is not an easy one. God is in no hurry to keep his promises. Instead we are challenged by famines, when our needs appear greater than God's supply. Or we face enemy coalitions that seem too strong for us to defeat. Judging by our circumstances, God's plan often makes little sense, as foolish as choosing a barren, elderly woman to bear the promised child or as senseless as bringing victory through a cross. Our challenges are often most fierce just after a great moment of spiritual success. At times God becomes silent when we need him most. At other times it is not his silence that we find challenging but his words. Throughout the centuries, God's people have encountered a side of God that looks more foreign than familiar, more ominous than comforting, more enemy than friend.

One effect of facing such challenges is the realization that we cannot walk this road of faith without God's help. Our best efforts are not good enough; in fact, they sometimes make matters worse. Our efforts are usually hindered because we give our fears too much freedom. The good news is that in our weakness, God proves his strength. God allows us to experience challenges so we will learn to walk by faith. When we do, he turns our failures into blessings, as he did in Abraham's encounters with Pharaoh and Abimelek. When we trust him, not images of him or feelings about him or past experiences with him, but trust God alone, even a God we don't fully understand, he proves himself faithful.

True faith produces obedience, and this is what God wants. Abraham needed to leave Harran to demonstrate that his faith was alive.

ABRAHAM: FATHER OF ALL WHO BELIEVE

He needed to refuse the king of Sodom to prove his trust was in God not in humans. At times the call for obedience seemed puzzling, as when Abraham complained of having no heir (Gen. 15:2–3). At other times it was devastating, as at Mount Moriah (ch. 22).

Through our faith and obedience, we become God's partner. He works his will through our work. However, it is not the case that we contribute 50 percent of the whole and God brings the other half. God chooses to work through us to bring about his plan. He has placed his talents into our hands and expects us to use them for his purposes, and he will demand an accounting (Matt. 25:14–30).

The one act of obedience that God demanded of both Abraham and all his offspring was the initiatory rite of circumcision. Jesus and the early church continued this demand, although they modified the initiatory rite from circumcision to baptism. In this way, Abraham serves as our prototype because baptism is now the irreplaceable mark of entry into God's covenant community. When we put our trust in God, trust that is proven genuine through our obedience, God counts us as righteous. This is why "those who have faith are children of Abraham" and "those who rely on faith are blessed along with Abraham, the man of faith" (Gal. 3:7, 9). No ritual can replace the need for a living faith. "It was not through law that Abraham and his offspring received the promise that he would be heir of the world," wrote Paul, "but through the righteousness that comes by faith" (Rom. 4:13).

As Abraham discovered, the challenges involved in this life of faith are "light and momentary troubles" that are "achieving for us an eternal glory that far outweighs them all" (2 Cor. 4:17). By following faithfully, Abraham became the father of many nations whose descendants outnumber the dust of the earth, the sand on the beach, and the stars in the sky. By faith we anticipate "an inheritance that can never perish, spoil or fade . . . kept in heaven" (1 Pet. 1:4).

EXAMPLE OF HOW TO WALK BY FAITH

Like a good father, Abraham left footprints to guide his spiritual children in the walk of faith. Although he was not perfect, he set the standard of what it means to believe. When summoned by God, he left his security and identity behind and entrusted himself and his family to an unseen and relatively unknown God. When God summons us out into deep water or dark woods, Abraham's example encourages us to obey.

Abraham had a courageous faith. Upon entering Canaan, he publicly proclaimed his commitment to Yahweh. Although he was just a new believer, he was willing to stand alone (Gen. 12:8). When powerful enemies threatened, without hesitation Abraham attacked and won a great victory (14:1–16). It took courage to refuse the reward offered by the king of Sodom and to negotiate with God on behalf of others. The opposite of faith is not doubt but fear. Through faith, courage replaces fear, as Abraham clearly demonstrated.

The writer of Hebrews defined faith as "confidence in what we hope for and assurance about what we do not see" (Heb. 11:1). This is the kind of faith Abraham showed, which is one reason he receives so much attention in the Hall of the Heroes of Faith (Heb. 11). Although he lived in tents as a nomad, he was certain of an invisible city "whose architect and builder is God" (Heb. 11:10). Unlike Lot who chose the fertile land near Sodom, Abraham remained in the heart of Canaan, trusting God to provide. He saw the blessings of God even before they arrived. He was confident he would hold Sarah's son in his arms, even though they were both too old to produce a child. He was confident in the resurrection of Isaac, even though the idea of resurrection was all but unknown in his day. To walk by faith, we must have something better than 20/20 vision.

Confident in God's promises, we must be able to see both what is invisible and what is yet to be.

Abraham provides an example of living with uncertainty. God told him to follow but didn't tell him where they were going. God made several promises but nothing happened for a long time. God's timetable is not ours. He does not speak on command. He does not act according to our understanding. If he did, he would not be God. Those who follow God must, like Abraham, learn to live with uncertainty. This is not uncertainty about whether God will act but about precisely how and when.

In Abraham we see a wonderful example of a person who put his faith in God and not in his own understanding of God. Had he been of the latter type, he would have reacted with disbelief or confusion when he heard Melchizedek equate Yahweh with El Elyon (Gen. 14:18–20). He would have denied that God had revealed himself to Hagar, an Egyptian slave girl running from her mistress. Had Abraham leaned on his own understanding, he would have missed the opportunity to intercede for Sodom; after all, who was he to negotiate with God? Abram would have refused to believe that God had visited Abimelek or that the king's subjects had any reverence for God. If Abraham's faith had been in the God of his own understanding, he never would have taken Isaac to Mount Moriah because God's command could not be reconciled with God's promise. However, Abraham's faith was in God, not in his faith in God or his experiences with God. For this reason, Abraham's faith was able to expand to fit his new circumstances. A living faith is a growing faith. The living faith of a young believer will be a withered skeleton in the believer's later years unless it grows to encompass new circumstances. If our faith is in the eternal God whose ways are "beyond tracing out" (Rom. 11:33), only eternity will provide sufficient room for our faith to expand.

Abraham possessed a loyal faith. His departure from Harran marked a break from any old loyalties and a commitment to follow Yahweh. He reaffirmed that loyalty many times, one in particular being the moment when he painfully marked himself and all the males of his household with the sign of the covenant (Gen. 17). That loyalty was tested many times, but none more severely than on Mount Moriah (ch. 22). He refused to put any other "gods" before Yahweh, not even this boy who represented everything precious in his life.

For the believer, every day brings challenges to our ultimate loyalty. At times those challenges come in the form of difficulties that force us to choose whether to trust in our own strength, or cast our anxiety upon God (1 Pet. 5:7). At other times those challenges come in the form of God's blessings. In that case, the challenge is whether we will trust more in those blessings than the One who provided them. Then there are the in-between challenges, when the everyday sameness of life lulls us into carelessness. Like our spiritual father Abraham, let us "walk before" almighty God "and be blameless" (Gen. 17:1), regardless of the challenges.

Abraham's faith remained strong to the end of his life. Believers of retirement age may be tempted to retire from an active faith. Although we would never consider turning away from God altogether, we may be tempted to take our foot off the accelerator and coast to life's conclusion. Believing that we have enough faith capital deposited in our account, we may attempt to live off the interest. This can happen in response to the physical and emotional challenges that accompany aging or as a response to a crisis that seems to demand more of us than we can give.

Although our spiritual father experienced great challenges, he did not waver in his faith. In spite of the death of his wife, the challenge of securing land for a burial plot, and the difficulty of finding the right wife for Isaac through whom the covenant would continue,

Abraham continued to trust God. Abraham walked with God right up to the moment when he "breathed his last and died at a good old age, an old man and full of years; and he was gathered to his people" (25:8). In his good death, as in his life, Abraham provided a worthy example to follow.

CONCLUSION

Those of us blessed with godly fathers understand the precious gift they represent. Their example and wise counsel make it easier for us to live our lives as a blessing to others. Even if your own father was not the good example you might have wished for, perhaps you are privileged to know surrogate fathers, men who stepped into your life to provide what your father did not or could not. Whatever may be true of our earthly or surrogate fathers, God has given us a father in Abraham. As Christians, we represent the fulfillment of the promise made to Abraham: that through his offspring, all nations of the earth would be blessed. As the apostle Paul wrote, God "redeemed us in order that the blessing given to Abraham might come to the Gentiles through Christ Jesus, so that by faith we might receive the promise of the Spirit" (Gal. 3:14). Abraham fathered our faith by pioneering God's redemptive plan. Our own walk of faith reflects the pattern of his life. Like a good father, he has left us footprints that we can follow.

Notes

CHAPTER 1

1. Dietrich Bonhoeffer, *The Cost of Discipleship* (New York: Touchstone, 1995), 89.

2. Gordon J. Wenham, *Genesis 1–15*, Word Biblical Commentary (Dallas: Word, 1987), 279.

CHAPTER 2

1. Victor H. Matthews and Don C. Benjamin, eds., "Visions of Neferti," *Old Testament Parallels: Laws and Stories from the Ancient Near East*, 3rd ed. (New York/Mahwah, NJ: Paulist Press, 2006), 337.

2. James B. Pritchard, ed., "Texts from the Tomb of General Hor-em-heb," *Ancient Near Eastern Texts: Relating to the Old Testament with Supplement*, 3rd ed. (Princeton, NJ: Princeton University Press, 1969), 251.

3. Louis Ginzberg, *The Legends of the Jews*, trans. Henrietta Szold, vol. 1 (Philadelphia: The Jewish Publication Society of America, 1968), 224.

CHAPTER 3

1. Steven Collins, "Where Is Sodom? The Case for Tall el-Hammam," *Biblical Archaeology Review* 39, no. 2 (March/April): 32–41, 70–71.

CHAPTER 4

1. Steven Collins, "Where Is Sodom? The Case for Tall el-Hammam," *Biblical Archaeology Review* 39, no. 2 (March/April): 32–41, 70–71.

2. Gordon J. Wenham, *Genesis 1–15*, Word Biblical Commentary (Dallas: Word, 1987), 308.

3. John E. Hartley, *Genesis*, New International Biblical Commentary (Peabody, MA: Hendrickson, 2000), 152.

4. E. A. Speiser, *Genesis*, The Anchor Bible (New York: Doubleday, 1964), 99.

5. Umberto Cassuto, *A Commentary on the Book of Exodus*, trans. Israel Abrahams (Jerusalem: The Magnes Press, 1967), 13. Such nomads are referred to outside the Bible as *apiru*, a term which sounds similar to the term *Hebrew*, but is linguistically unrelated.

6. James H. Charlesworth, ed. and D. R. Darnell, trans., "A Prayer of Praise to God for His Greatness, and for His Appointment of Leaders for His People," *The Old Testament Pseudepigrapha*, vol. 2 (New York: Doubleday, 1985), 688.

7. See 2 Enoch 71:28–30. James H. Charlesworth, ed. and F. I. Anderson, trans., *The Old Testament Pseudepigrapha*, vol. 1 (New York: Doubleday, 1983), 208.

8. Hartley, *Genesis*, 153.

9. Yahweh Most High (YHWH Elyon): Psalm 7:17; 47:2; 97:9. God Most High (El Elyon): Psalm 78:35. Most High (Elyon): Numbers 24:16; Deuteronomy 32:8; Isaiah 14:14. Yahweh used parallel with Most High: Psalm 9:1–2; 18:13; 21:7; 83:18; 91:9; 92:1.

10. Derek Kidner, *Genesis*, Tyndale Old Testament Commentaries (Downers Grove, IL: InterVarsity Press, 1967), 120.

11. Ibid., 121.

CHAPTER 5

1. Franz Delitzsch, *The First Book of Moses (Genesis)*, trans. James Martin (Grand Rapids, MI: Eerdmans, 1951), 210.

2. Gordon J. Wenham, *Genesis 1–15*, Word Biblical Commentary (Dallas: Word, 1987), 334.

3. Ibid., 335.

CHAPTER 7

1. Gordon J. Wenham, *Genesis 1–15*, Word Biblical Commentary (Dallas: Word, 1987), 20.

2. Gordon J. Wenham, *Genesis 16–50*, Word Biblical Commentary (Dallas: Word Books, 1994), 16.

CHAPTER 8

1. Gordon J. Wenham, *Genesis 16–50*, Word Biblical Commentary (Dallas: Word Books, 1994), 48.

2. E. A. Speiser, *Genesis*, The Anchor Bible (New York: Doubleday, 1964), 132.

3. Derek Kidner, *Genesis*, Tyndale Old Testament Commentaries (Downers Grove, IL: InterVarsity Press, 1967), 132.

CHAPTER 9

1. Wilbur Glenn Williams, *Genesis: A Bible Commentary in the Wesleyan Tradition* (Indianapolis: Wesleyan Publishing House, 2000), 163.

CHAPTER 10

1. Derek Kidner, *Genesis*, Tyndale Old Testament Commentaries (Downers Grove, IL: InterVarsity Press, 1967), 139.

2. Jubilees 17:4, O. S. Wintermute, trans., *The Old Testament Pseudepigrapha*, vol. 2, 90.

3. Kidner, *Genesis*, 140.

4. Gordon J. Wenham, *Genesis 16–50*, Word Biblical Commentary (Dallas: Word Books, 1994), 77.

CHAPTER 11

1. Gordon J. Wenham, *Genesis 16–50*, Word Biblical Commentary (Dallas: Word Books, 1994), 104.

2. John E. Hartley, *Genesis*, New International Biblical Commentary (Peabody, MA: Hendrickson, 2000), 207.

3. Ibid., 208.

4. Ephraim Syrus, "Hymn VI," trans. J. B. Morris, *Hymns on the Nativity*, *Nicene and Post-Nicene Fathers*, vol. 13, 2nd series (Peabody, MA: Hendrickson, 2004), 239.

5. Derek Kidner, *Genesis*, Tyndale Old Testament Commentaries (Downers Grove, IL: InterVarsity Press, 1967), 144.

6. Søren Kierkegaard, *Fear and Trembling*, trans. Walter Lowrie (Princeton: Princeton University Press, 1941), 27.

7. John Calvin, *Institutes of the Christian Religion*, 1:568, cited in Wenham, *Genesis 16–50*, 109.

8. Ambrose, "Duties of the Clergy, Book I," *Nicene and Post-Nicene Fathers*, vol. 10, 2nd series, ed. Philip Schaff (Peabody, MA: Hendrickson, 2004), 12.

9. Wenham, *Genesis 16–50*, 111.

CHAPTER 12

1. Gordon J. Wenham, *Genesis 16–50*, Word Biblical Commentary (Dallas: Word Books, 1994), 126.

2. Derek Kidner, *Genesis*, Tyndale Old Testament Commentaries (Downers Grove, IL: InterVarsity Press, 1967), 145.

3. Wenham, *Genesis 16–50*, 128.

4. Ibid., 142, citing Genesis 31:24, 29; Exodus 34:12; and Deuteronomy 4:9.

5. E. A. Speiser, *Genesis*, The Anchor Bible (New York: Doubleday, 1964), 183.

6. Wenham, *Genesis 16–50*, 145.

7. John E. Hartley, *Genesis*, New International Biblical Commentary (Peabody, MA: Hendrickson, 2000), 224.

8. Wenham, *Genesis 16–50*, citing rabbinic sources.

9. Kidner, *Genesis*, 149.

10. Ibid., 150.

11. Walter Brueggemann, *Genesis*, Interpretation: A Bible Commentary for Teaching and Preaching (Atlanta: John Knox Press, 2010), 201.

12. Ibid., 202.

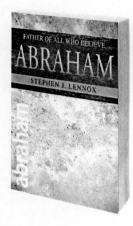
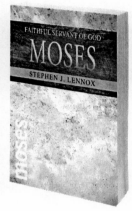
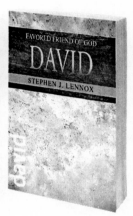

CPSIA information can be obtained
at www.ICGtesting.com
Printed in the USA
FFOW05n0314121115